On Stage with Lata

Born in Fatehpur (Shekhawati), Rajasthan, in 1943, **Mohan Deora** moved to America in 1964. He has a master's degree in chemical engineering and an MBA and has worked for thirty-five years with DTE Energy at their Nuclear Power Plant Fermi-2. From 1975 to 1998, Deora and his team organized over a hundred path-breaking Lata Mangeshkar concerts in the US, Canada, West Indies and Fiji. He is now retired and lives in Florida.

Born in Mumbai, **Rachana Shah** was a child singer and performed on stage with her aunt Lata Mangeshkar in various countries. She graduated from St Xavier's College in political science in 1988. She has worked on the Marathi stage and for six years was the media head for the celebrated photographer Gautam Rajadhyaksha. Rachana lives in Mumbai and is married to ENT surgeon Dr Nishit Shah.

Born in India, **Nasreen Munni Kabir** is a London-based film-maker and author who has made dozens of documentaries on Hindi cinema and written sixteen books on the subject. Kabir has served a six-year term as governor on the board of the British Film Institute and continues to curate the annual Indian film season on UK's Channel 4 TV.

Mohan Deora

Rachana Shah

On Stage with Lata

Mohan Deora
Rachana Shah

Introduction by
Lata Mangeshkar

Edited by
Nasreen Munni Kabir

HarperCollins *Publishers* India

First published in India in 2017 by
HarperCollins *Publishers* India

Copyright © Mohan Deora, Rachana Shah 2017

P-ISBN: 978-93-5264-316-5
E-ISBN: 978-93-5264-317-2

2 4 6 8 10 9 7 5 3 1

Mohan Deora and Rachana Shah assert the moral right
to be identified as the authors of this work.

HarperCollins *Publishers*

A-75, Sector 57, Noida, Uttar Pradesh 201301, India
1 London Bridge Street, London, SE1 9GF, United Kingdom
Hazelton Lanes, 55 Avenue Road, Suite 2900, Toronto, Ontario M5R 3L2
and 1995 Markham Road, Scarborough, Ontario M1B 5M8, Canada
25 Ryde Road, Pymble, Sydney, NSW 2073, Australia
195 Broadway, New York, NY 10007, USA

Typeset in 13/15 Arno Pro at
SŪRYA, New Delhi

Printed and bound at
Thomson Press (India) Ltd

For my parents
Kashiprashad and Champadevi

– Mohan Deora

Contents

Contents

Preface

Different aspects of Lata Mangeshkar's life, her professional career and her social and charitable activities have been the subject of many books and articles. But a feature of her working life that has remained largely undocumented are her international tours and pioneering role in raising the standard of Hindi film music concerts in the West.

I am proud and privileged to say that together with my team, we organized and promoted Lata Mangeshkar's shows in the United States of America, Canada, the Caribbean and the Fiji Islands from 1975 to 1998. The shows were all record-breaking events and had her fans coming in their thousands to see her at every venue and in every city.

Lata Mangeshkar was undoubtedly instrumental in upping the bar of the Hindi film music show outside India. Formerly, singers would perform in low-key song-and-dance events that were held in small community halls, schools and colleges. But Lataji insisted that she and her co-artists would sing in mainstream venues. She was the first Indian singer to take the stage at the Royal Albert Hall in London (1974), and during our US/Canada tours, she sang at the top venues where world-class musicians have performed. These prestigious venues included New York's Carnegie Hall, Madison Square Garden (MSG), Shrine Auditorium Los Angeles [LA], Fox Theater (Detroit) and Maple Leaf Gardens (Toronto).

In late 1974, when I first proposed the idea of touring the USA and Canada to her, she refused. It was only thanks to Mukeshji's gentle persuasion that Lataji finally agreed. From the first tour in 1975, we went onto make musical history for our communities settled in the West.

For many years, I have believed that the experience and memories of those concerts should be preserved in book form. That said, I was a little nervous when discussing the idea with Lataji, as I did not know how she would react. But when I explained the kind of book I had in mind, she immediately encouraged me by saying that she thought it was an excellent idea. That's all I needed to hear.

It took me about two years to gather the material and images needed for the book. My core team and I spent several hours recollecting memories of those times, reliving those wonderfully special days when we put the shows together. As soon as I had gathered all the material and notes that I had made along the way, I sat down to writing. It was not long before I realized that I needed the help of Rachana Shah, Lataji's niece. Although this book is written entirely in the first person narrative, I would not have been able to complete it without her help. I have known Rachana since she was nine years old, and when I told her that I wanted us to share the author credit, she was reluctant, and said, 'No, Uncle. It is not necessary.' But I was adamant.

On Stage with Lata is the result of our collaboration. Through anecdotes and memories, this is an account of Lata Mangeshkar on tour, starting with our first show at the beautiful Shrine Auditorium in Los Angeles on 9 May 1975 when Lataji and Mukeshji topped the bill.

Beyond the confines of a recording booth, or as a voice coming from the lips of generations of screen stars, we discovered a whole other side of Lataji as she performed before her army of adoring fans. Her perfect dedication towards her work, her exchanges with co-singers, musicians and friends provide new insight into a personality whose brilliant songs are etched forever in our hearts. The overwhelming response to Lataji in the Fiji Islands or in the Caribbean came as a surprise even to her – but as always she reacted to the wildly enthusiastic reception she received with great humility.

Over a twenty-three-year period of touring, each set of concerts brought new adventures – it was a very different kind of musical journey for us all. Many things happened along the way, but the most devastating was losing Mukeshji in Detroit in 1976. We could not get over his sad demise.

To organize fifty concerts across the USA and Canada was no simple task. It required detailed planning and commitment. I had my responsibilities to my own professional career as a nuclear power generation specialist, so I needed support from my friends. They had their own day jobs too, but together we somehow accomplished our mission. My core team stood by me through the years and without their help, these concerts would not have happened. It is impossible to list the great number of well-wishers who came forward to solve our problems, but they know that I shall always be in their debt.

In undertaking this book, I have used the generous contributions of many people who were closely associated with me, starting with my 1975 tour partner Ramesh Shishu. I would like to mention the Detroit journalist Usha Mangrulkar who was once a newscaster for the radio programme *The Sound of India*, and whose long article on the 1975 tour was of immense help to me.

I am very grateful to Nasreen Munni Kabir who has so meticulously edited the text, translated the Hindi passages and helped Rachana and me give the book its final shape. I extend my thanks to my brother Ashok and his wife Alka, Vishakha, Ron Eisenberg, my three grandchildren Ajay, Saaniya, Armaan, and Shantanu Ray Chaudhuri of HarperCollins who have encouraged me all the way.

If I were to thank Lata Mangeshkar for putting her trust in me over all these years, and for all the many things that she has done for me, I am sure this book would double in size. So I will end by saying that there is nothing truer than the simple statement made by my wife Suvarna, my children Aparna and Sunit, and all the people who came forward to help when they said, 'Anything for Lataji.'

MOHAN DEORA

Introduction

One day some concert organizers came to my father and asked if they could hold a jalsa where my father Deenanath Mangeshkar, a celebrated classical singer, would perform. I was standing nearby and overheard the conversation. I said, 'Baba, I want to sing too.'

'What will you sing?' he asked.

'You taught me Raga Khambavati, so I'll sing that, and a song from one of your plays.'

He looked at me somewhat taken aback – perhaps my confidence took him by surprise. I was only nine years old. My father thought it over for a few minutes and agreed that I could sing with him on the stage.

Later that day, I put on a white frock with tiny patterns on it, styled my hair in a wave across one side of my face, and started to head towards the main door of the house when my mother stopped me and asked where I was going. I didn't answer her and quickly slipped out. There was a photographer's studio across the street from where we lived. I pushed my way in and asked the photographer to take a picture of me. A few days later, it appeared in the local newspaper alongside a photograph of my father, with the caption: 'Classical programme by father and daughter'.

The evening of the concert finally arrived. I was the first to get onto the stage and sang Raga Khambavati. Then my father sang late into the evening. I was very sleepy and put my head on his lap and fell fast asleep. Everyone seemed happy enough about my first public appearance.

My father, who was a very good astrologer, once read my horoscope. He told my mother, 'Lata is a very good singer. You cannot imagine how famous she will become. She will sing but will not marry.' His words did come true and music became the centre of my life.

I am sure that performing on the stage at that young age helped me to sing in public. Over the years, I have sung at many concerts in India, especially in Kolkata. We sang in theatres and stadiums. The Bengali audience was fantastic. They listened so attentively. They usually asked me to sing the Bengali songs that I had recorded.

Sometimes strange things would happen at concerts. Someone would come to the green room and ask, 'May I sing in your show?' I would refuse and say, 'If you want to sing, sing for me. If you sing well, you can rehearse and sing on stage. But I cannot just let you start performing in our show without knowing what you can do.' This kind of thing happened in India and even when I performed abroad.

My first concert outside India was in 1974 at the Royal Albert Hall in London. It was a wonderful show. A close friend, S.N. Gourisaria, and the celebrated diplomat and statesman, V.K. Krishna Menon, who had launched the

India League in London, organized the show beautifully. Dilip Kumar introduced me in glowing words, but when I stepped onto the stage and faced the audience, I felt a trembling sensation in my throat. I could not utter a sound. I did not know what to do. I knew it was the daunting pressure of getting it right. I somehow sang the opening shloka and by the time I had finished singing, I had become a tigress!

In late 1974, Mukesh Bhaiya came to see me and talked about Mohan Deora who lived in Detroit. He said Mr Deora had organized concerts for him and now wanted to produce a Lata Mangeshkar tour of the US and Canada. I was hesitant about singing in America. In 1969, when I was visiting my close friend Nalini Mhatre who lived in Canada, she thought it would be fun if we went to New York for a few days. In later years, I came to love New York and it became my favourite US city, but at first, I found it scary and intimidating. The hotel where we were staying was very rough: it was not a nice place at all. Rather odd-looking people milled around, and at nights we could hear loud and aggressive banging on the doors. I got scared and told Nalini we should go back to Canada at once. This unfortunate experience coloured my first impression of America.

Mukesh Bhaiya was aware that I was reluctant to perform in the US, but he insisted I should at least meet Mohan Deora. So Mohanji came to Mumbai in December 1974. To be perfectly honest, when I met him I was not sure that he and his team would be able to organize the shows well. That was my first impression. But Mukesh Bhaiya said Mohanji was a very good man and a good organizer. He said he was happy with his US shows and assured me that everything would go well. I thought it over and finally agreed. 'Mukesh Bhaiya, if you come with me, I'll go,' I said.

'Of course I'll come with you. It'll be something new and exciting for the audience there if we went together.'

I was unaware at first that I had in fact a connection to Mohan Deora's family through his wife, Suvarna, whom I call Bhabhi. She was the daughter of the very famous director P.L. Santoshi, who also wrote lyrics. Santoshi Saab was very fond of me and once came to me saying that he was planning to make a movie with Madhubala and wanted me to compose the music. He even sent me some lyrics, but I explained that I had so much work and did not have the time to compose. I think the movie was shelved and then I believe Madhubala also got busy with another film.

I did not choose the auditoriums for the US/Canada tours. But I did tell Mohanji that considering my first show abroad was at the Royal Albert Hall, we had to find venues of the same calibre. I did not want to perform in a community hall or in a school or something. That's where some of the earlier performances of playback singers had taken place abroad.

Kishore-da once told me about a show in a cinema hall in Southall, London. He was singing 'Koi humdum na raha koi sahaara na raha' [I have no one to love or someone to depend upon] when a totally drunk fellow staggered onto the stage, put his head on Kishore-da's shoulders and started sobbing loudly. Kishore-da got a terrible fright. 'What's going on here?' The organizer rushed forward and took the man away. Then someone shouted rudely, 'Now sing us "*Mere sapnon ki raani*".' It must have been a Punjabi fan who probably adored Kishore-da, but instead of making him feel appreciated, he managed to alarm Kishore-da even further.

With this story in mind, I thought to myself what I would do if these kinds of things happened to me in America. I was confident of the audience in London. I always liked London, and still do, so I did not hesitate to sing there. But I was unsure of the American audience. Would there be whistles and catcalls? I didn't know what to expect. That's why I said to Mohanji, 'Look, I've sung at the Royal Albert Hall, so my shows must take place in good venues.' And Mohanji did find the best venues for us in the US and Canada, and that made a big difference.

Before we arrived in the US, the musicians and I rehearsed many times in India. We also rehearsed at the venue itself during the morning of the show. I would check the mic position and do a sound test. The first show of the 1975 tour took place at the Shrine Auditorium in Los Angeles on Friday, 9 May. It went extremely well. A few days later we performed at Maple Leaf Gardens in Toronto. It was another amazing show. The audience was so generous in their appreciation, and showered us with love.

Once during the tour, some US-born young Indian boys came to Mukesh Bhaiya and insisted that he accept an invitation to dine out. At first he was reluctant, but they somehow persuaded him and off they went. At the end of the evening, when the bill was presented to them, each of the boys took out $10 from their wallets to pay. They were planning to go Dutch. All this seemed very odd to Mukesh Bhaiya who thought they were collecting money for a donation or something. He felt very uncomfortable, so he insisted on paying the whole bill. It was not a small amount by any means. When Mukesh Bhaiya returned to the hotel, he came to tell me about the evening. As he was heading to his room, he said: 'Didi, I won't be accepting any invitations for dinner again.' We both had a good laugh.

The third city in our 1975 tour was San Francisco. We landed there on 11 May, and from the airport I went straight to the hotel, changed and by 4 p.m. I was at the Oakland Auditorium Arena. I always made it a point to arrive at the venue at least an hour before the show, and then I would sit quietly in the green room. On the other hand, Mukesh Bhaiya, like Raj Kapoor and Dilip Kumar, had this habit of coming late. We waited for him but he did not show up. I was not sure if we should carry on waiting for him because he was supposed to introduce me on the stage.

The hall was packed. It was 5.30 and still no sign of Mukesh Bhaiya. Everyone looked at me for a decision. I told Ramesh Shishu, Mohan Deora's tour partner, to announce that we were starting. Without the usual introduction, I sang the shloka and then proceeded to sing three songs. By that time, Mukesh Bhaiya had arrived. I could see him watching me from the wings. He looked very sheepish and embarrassed.

When it came to the presentation of the show itself, I was definite about some things. For example, I did not want any of us singers to wear garish clothes, big earrings or excessive jewellery. I wanted simplicity. We had to look like singers, not like glamorous movie stars. What the audiences liked, I think, was that we were dressed simply. When Mukesh Bhaiya sang, he was not wearing a silver-threaded or sequinned jacket. It looks dreadful anyway. If we were dancers, watch us dance. But we are singers, and I wanted the audience to listen to our singing.

To keep the audience entertained, we presented a variety of voices. I would sing three or four songs, then Mukesh Bhaiya sang. Once he was done, we would sing a few duets. Then Usha would come on, and I might sing a duet with her. I usually started the second half of the show and sang the last song. My sister Usha, my nephews and my niece Rachana, who was only nine then, would also sing. Rachana still sings very well and can sing classical music. Asha's son, Anand, came with us for some shows but he did not sing.

A basic rule about stage performance is that the singer should know the song lines perfectly. Some singers would end up singing the wrong words if they had forgotten the lyrics; this should not happen. As far as the selection of songs was concerned, we had a sense of what was popular in both the United States of America and Canada. We also chose songs that worked well on the stage. I made it a point to sing a medley in different languages – Bengali, Marathi, Assamese, Gujarati. I would tell the audience that I had prepared the medley especially for them. It is always heart-warming to hear your mother tongue, especially if you are living in a far-off country.

There were some songs that people liked, and I didn't, but I had to sing them, like *'Bindiya chamkegi*. I never liked that song even when I had first recorded it. The songs the audience really loved were the haunting melodies like '*Aayega aanewala*', '*Kahin deep jale*', '*Ajaa re pardesi*' and '*Naina barse rhim jhim rhim jhim*'. When it came to the duets with Mukesh Bhaiya, people enjoyed '*Saawan ka mahina*'. I think it amused them because in the song Mukesh Bhaiya has to teach me how to pronounce the word 'sor'.

After the last show in 1975, Mohanji organized a dinner for us all in a good Indian restaurant. The restaurant staff had set up a long table on the first floor for us. We were quite a few and Raj Kapoor also decided to join us. When Raj Kapoor arrived, he said with great gusto, 'Open the champagne!' So the champagne bottle was opened. Everyone was offered a glass. Raj Kapoor looked at me and could see that I was feeling very uncomfortable. There was a friend sitting next to me, so he came to her and said, 'You live in New York, you can have a drink.' This friend of mine was scared of me and immediately said, 'No, no, no, I don't want any champagne.' I told her, 'You're used to having a drink, go ahead. But I won't drink.' Then Raj Saab came to my side and said, 'Stop scaring people, Lata! Let them be. They are terrified of you and that's why they're not drinking champagne!' I was laughing inside, but did not say a word. But it was true – Mohanji and the others were not drinking because I was there.

The first US–Canada tour was very joyful in every way, but disaster struck in 1976 when we went back to America. Mukesh Bhaiya and his son Nitin were staying on the floor above mine in our Detroit hotel. At five one evening, I got a call from the hotel reception saying, 'Mr Mukesh has suffered a heart attack.' He was immediately taken to hospital and we rushed over there. Mohanji arrived just when the doctor came to tell us that Mukeshji was no more. I felt as though all my strength had left me. I sat on the sofa in the waiting area, numb. My brother Hridaynath went to the auditorium and broke the news to the Detroit audience that we were cancelling the show. We refunded the ticket money. A week or so later, I came back to Mumbai and went to see Mukesh Bhaiya's family. It was a shocking thing for us to lose him. I was very close to him. I called him my brother and believed that he was a real brother to me.

As time passed, we developed new ideas for the shows. We thought audiences would love to see some of their favourite stars on stage with us. So, for the New York show in 1980, a friend of mine and I met Amitabhji at the Willingdon Club in Mumbai to request him to come to America. He immediately agreed. I asked him if he could sing, and when he said that he could, I encouraged him to sing on stage.

I was very moved to hear that the minute Amitabhji and Jayaji had landed in New York, instead of going to relax at their hotel, they went directly to Sloan Kettering Hospital to see Nargisji. They knew she was ill and was being treated for cancer.

Our New York show was held at Felt Forum where Amitabh Bachchan sang '*Mere angne mein*', and when he came to the line '*jiski biwi chhoti uska bhi bada naam hai*', he asked Jayaji to join him on stage. When she stepped onto the podium, he carried her in his arms. The audience went wild with joy.

Some months later, I read an interview in which Amitabhji said that he had sung for the first time in public because I had asked him to. He added that our musical concerts had given him the idea of doing his own shows in America. Mohanji later told me how extremely popular and good they were. I am grateful to Amitabhji for coming to New York for our show, and for mentioning the fact that I had encouraged him to sing in public.

In 1985, Kishore-da accompanied me on tour. The audience loved our duets, especially '*Gaata rahe mera dil*' and '*Kora kaagaz tha ye mann mera*'. This time we asked Sunil Dutt to be part of the show and he graciously agreed. In fact, Kishore-da and Sunilji created an impromptu comic act. Kishore Kumar had played Sunil Dutt's singing guru in *Padosan*, so

Kishore-da pranced onto the stage calling out, 'Bhole, Bhole!' (Sunil Dutt's character's name in the film). From the other corner of the stage, Sunil Dutt cried, 'Guru, Guru!' Kishore-da then proceeded to sing '*Mere saamne waale khidki mein*' while Sunilji stood at a microphone, lip-synching. The audience were beside themselves with laughter. It was hilarious.

Kishore-da would talk a lot between songs. I remember during the Toronto show, he said, 'Let us sing the duet that you don't like, and I don't like either.' I was silent, wondering which song he was talking about. Then he said, 'We'll sing "*Chai pe bulaaya hai*". I know you don't like that song, do you?' I did not reply. I really did not like the song and had in fact told him that we should not sing it. But he often surprised me and did all sorts of crazy things. It was a wonderful experience working with Kishore-da. We had so much fun together on the stage. I remember Kishore-da requested Mohanji to take a picture of the sign outside Madison Square Garden. It was a moment of great pride for us all to see a

Lata Mangeshkar arrives in Los Angeles on 2 May 1975 for the first
US/Canada tour. Bouquet presented to her by Mitul Shishu and Aparna Deora.

Pandit Nehru looks on as P.L. Santoshi receives an award for his film *Hum Panchhi
Ek Daal Ke* from President Rajendra Prasad.

Lata Mangeshkar and her family arrive at the Detroit airport for the 1980 tour.

Mukesh, who initially persuaded Lata Mangeshkar to agree to the concert tour, arrives in Los Angeles with his daughter Neelam. May 1975.

Packed house at the Kennedy Center for the Performing Arts, Washington, D.C. 19 May 1975.

A rush of emotion filled the venue when Lata Mangeshkar and Mukesh sang their memorable duets. Civic Opera House, Chicago. 23 May 1975.

The tours took Lata Mangeshkar to many US and Canadian cities between 1975 and 1998. Everywhere she sang, she was received with standing ovations.

Lata Mangeshkar and family prepare for the next show. The Mangeshkars (l to r): Bharathi, Usha, Hridaynath, Lata with Anil Mohile and Mohan Deora (standing).

During the early tours, Lata Mangeshkar had little time to sightsee. On the insistence of her family, she visited Disneyland with Mohan Deora and his wife Suvarna.

Lata Mangeshkar rehearsing in her suite at Hilton Hotel. 8 May 1975. Arranger and composer Anil Mohile on the harmonium.

Manna Dey expressed his surprise at the detailed planning of each show. Detroit's Ford Auditorium. 19 September 1980.

The first concert of the 1975 tour was held at Los Angeles's Shrine Auditorium on 9 May. It was a major event for the local South Asian community.

The revolving stage at the Valley Forge Auditorium, Philadelphia. 16 January 1977.

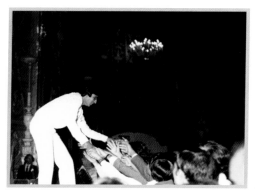

Amitabh Bachchan's fans could not get enough of their favourite star.
Felt Forum (MSG), New York. 20 September 1980.

On stage, the unpredictable Kishore Kumar even surprised Lata Mangeshkar with his off-the-cuff wit.

Kishore Kumar's comical opening speech was matched by his antics. Cobo Arena, Detroit. 16 June 1985.

Lata Mangeshkar with sister Usha Mangeshkar, Padmini Kolhapure and Dilip Kumar. The United Way charity show was held at the Maple Leaf Gardens, Toronto.

Dilip Kumar kept the audience spellbound when he introduced the show in Toronto. 9 June 1985.

Lata Mangeshkar's American and Canadian fans wrote in with their song requests. Seen at Mohan Deora's home in Troy, Michigan. July 1995.

माझी गीते

रहेना रहे ✓ २   आ आरे परदेसी २
क्यूं न बने ✓ =
ठंडी हवायें २
सखस् ✓ =
ओ सजना १०
(३) ये रात ये चांदनी १   ११
(१) ओ वसंती २
लग जा गले ३   कहारी मेरा
(६) नैना बरसे ४   चंद मसी बदन
भवरा ५   राधा ना बोले
(२) राधिके बलमा ५.   सारी सारी
उठाये जा उनके ५.
मेरे मेहबूब ११   रूप
ड्वाली वाले २ =   नूरी
जो वादा ✓   गायूं
(६) तेरे बिना ८   बड़े अरमानों से
(५) हाये रक्षा ९   = रूप
लिखे जो खत २ =
सुरनाल ✓
अपना मराठा
मैं तुलसी २ =
आज फिर २

Ramesh Shishu and Mohan Deora (right) finally sign the agreement for the concert tours in America and Canada.

Opening the first concert of the first tour with a shloka from the Bhagavadgita. 9 May 1975.

With Waheeda Rehman and sister Usha Mangeshkar. Nephew Adinath Mangeshkar and Sudesh Bhosle (back row) at the AAPI charity show. Fox Theater, Detroit. 1 October 1995.

Mohan Deora with Saira Banu and Dilip Kumar at the United Way charity event in Toronto. 9 June 1985.

show with Indian artists being sold out at that prestigious venue.

In the same year [1985] that Sunil Dutt appeared on our show, Dilip Kumar and Saira Banu had also graciously agreed to come. This was thanks to our common London friend S.N. Gourisaria. When I was told that Yusuf Bhai was coming, I wondered what he would do. We would be singing, but would he enjoy just listening to us? Then he appeared on stage and mesmerized the audience with his elegant way of speaking – he has such a gentle voice and such perfect Urdu.

Among the other film personalities who joined us singers were the novelist and poet, Padma Sachdev, and my niece Padmini Kolhapure, who was so lovely and charming. I asked Padma Sachdev to accompany us to America in 1977. She came without hesitation and introduced me in such generous terms. I remember it was a bitterly cold year and there was snow everywhere. There was a fountain in the garden of the hotel where we were staying.

Rachana, who was very young at the time, fell into the fountain. We were very scared for her. The poor child was frozen.

In 1998, I suggested to Mohanji that we invite the wonderful actor Farida Jalal, and he thought it was a very good idea. I was touched by her willingness to be part of the tour. She came with her husband, the actor Tabrez Barmavar, and introduced me on stage with kind and heartfelt words. Faridaji was particularly fond of my nephew Baijnath and loved his singing. He sang '*Jhule jhule lal dam mast kalandar*' so well that the audience always demanded an encore.

I cannot forget the sweetness of Waheeda Rehman. She is a lovely person and I have sung so many film songs for her. In 1995, when I heard that she was in Canada with her children who were studying there, I called her. Would she agree to introduce me on stage? We did not meet very often in India because we were both so busy, but the moment I put the question to her, without a moment's hesitation, she said yes. She was so dignified and graceful.

People have asked me if I have ever suffered from stage fright. I do not believe that I have, but I was fearful of making a mistake. So I would prepare myself mentally and give myself ample time. Two hours before the show, I'd choose the sari I was going to wear; sometimes I got ready in the hotel and sometimes I would change at the venue itself. Then I'd sit in the green room thinking that I had to sing well, people should not say that Lata was nervous or scared. I didn't want to hear people say, 'This went wrong, that went wrong.' What I wanted to hear was, 'Lata sang well.' It was the same thought I had whenever I recorded a playback song. It was not fear, rather the determination to get it right.

I was known for enunciating every word in a song. Everyone thought that the words I sang were always clear, and that I sang in tune. I was confident about that. When singing on stage, what was essential for me was to be able to hear the harmonium clearly – because it gave me the right pitch. So the arranger/conductor Anil Mohile stood near me as he played the harmonium. Sometimes a musician might go off-key – say a string was broken or he would play a wrong note – so I relied on the constant pitch of the harmonium. It was reassuring to me that Anil was close at hand.

Yesterday I came across an old photograph of Anil Mohile and I felt so sad. He died of a heart attack in his sleep in 2012. His wife was waiting for him to wake up that sad morning, and when the door to his room did not open, they realized something was wrong. He was a great support to me. He was an excellent arranger, conductor and composer as well.

The gratitude I still feel towards all the members of my team is beyond measure. The presentation of the shows was always of a high standard and that was also thanks to the master of ceremonies, Harish Bhimani, to whom I am very grateful.

The sound recordist Shashank Lalchand, who came with us on all the tours, was like my brother. At every concert, and in every venue, he made sure all the microphone positions were correct and all the technical problems resolved. Hridaynath and Shashank got on very well. They would sit together at the mixing desk to make sure the quality of sound would be as perfect as possible during the performance.

The backing singers were very good and all the musicians played beautifully. They were so dedicated and showed me so much affection. We worked hard, and we laughed a lot too. One year we happened to be in America at Diwali, and Mohanji decided to give all the musicians a gold coin each. It was a nice way to celebrate Diwali in a foreign land.

Madan Mohan's son Sanjeev Kohli and his wife Anju came with us for many shows. He would help with the stage direction and in every way he could. Sanjeev never charged a rupee. He has done everything for me from his heart. I used to call Madan Mohan my brother and so his son Sanjeev is like a son to me. And then there was the generous support of my co-singers, starting with Mukesh Bhaiya, Kishore-da, Manna Dey, Nitin Mukesh, S. Balasubramaniam, and many other talented singers. Thinking back to that time today, I know the tours would not have been possible without the kindness and help of so many, including my sisters Usha and Meena.

Most importantly there was the generosity of the audience. From 1975 to 1998, in every venue and country where I performed, even in Australia where I sang at the Sydney Opera House, people showered me with affection and appreciation. Performing for a live audience is an altogether different experience – it's all happening right there – it's alive. For years I had been recording songs in a small recording booth with only the composer, lyricist and film director to tell me if they thought the singing was good enough. The audiences at the concerts, in contrast, were made up of people from India, Pakistan and Bangladesh, who had settled in the USA and Canada for decades, and they came in thousands to the shows, applauding and encouraging us singers. I honestly did not expect the kind of reaction we got. Nor could I have ever imagined the tremendous love that I would receive in the Caribbean and in the Fiji Islands. It has been a deeply satisfying and humbling feeling to be so appreciated.

All my initial hesitations of performing in America and having Mohan Deora organize the shows vanished by the end of the first tour in 1975. I became very comfortable with Mohanji and his family. I started calling him Mohan Bhaiya. Despite having spent half his life in the US, he has remained very Indian. His eating habits, his way of speaking and thinking, his flaring up suddenly or being very calm – it's all very Indian. He is also a sensitive man. It was difficult to look at him when Mukesh Bhaiya died. Mohanji was completely ashen.

As the years passed, Mohan Bhaiya and I enjoyed working together and very quickly I started considering the Deora family and their children, Sunit and Aparna, as my own family. Whenever I travelled to Detroit, I stayed in their home, whether on tour or holiday. Bhabhi and I cooked together and shopped together. We spent hours in each other's company. I got on very well with Mohan Bhaiya and his brother Sajjan. We laughed a lot and joked around. Many people have asked me to do shows in America, but I felt a sense of loyalty to Mohan Deora because of our very close ties.

The first time we went together to Las Vegas was on Mukesh Bhaiya's insistence. Then it became a habit. Bhabhi and I would spend hours in the shopping malls in Vegas. I also thoroughly enjoyed playing the slot machines. I would go to one casino or another. Whatever money I won, the same coins would be put back into another slot machine. Sometimes I played throughout the night and at six the next morning, I'd make my way to the hotel/casino coffee shop and have a glass of cold milk, a toast, and some dollar pancakes with maple syrup.

One evening some Indians saw me playing the slot machine and looked shocked. 'Lataji likes the slot machine?' When I returned to India, a journalist called me up and said, 'I hear you enjoy gambling and you go to Las Vegas to gamble. I don't like it.' I got angry and said, 'It is not your father's money that I'm spending. I play with my own money.' He went silent. I was really annoyed. Was it a sin or something? I am not Mirabai or a saint. I am a human being and so what if I enjoyed playing the slot machines?

Another odd thing happened. One day in Las Vegas, I decided to wear a blue shalwar-kameez and a blue dupatta, although I usually wear saris. A few days later, a report appeared in an Indian newspaper: 'Lata was standing in front of a hotel casino. She was wearing blue jeans.' I thought to myself: 'Shaabaash!'

When Mohan Bhaiya told me that he and my niece Rachana were writing this book, I was very pleased to hear that the story behind the tours would be documented for the future. There are many books written on various aspects of Indian cinema, but few that have recorded the experience of playback singers performing on the international stage. Or that have given insight into the far-reaching impact of Indian film music on millions outside India. Hindi film songs continue to attract much love from people of other cultures.

We singers – Rafi Saab, Kishore-da, Mukesh Bhaiya, Manna Dey Saab, Talat Mahmood Saab, my sister Asha, Geeta Dutt and many others – have had the good fortune of bringing alive enchanting melodies with fine words that have been composed by our talented musicians and gifted lyricists over the decades. I believe our songs have helped millions of Indians settled all over the world to maintain a deep connection to the homeland.

When I think back to those times, there is one incident that I am unlikely to forget. I was in Trinidad on 28 September 1980. It was my fifty-first birthday. We had performed at the Jean Pierre Complex in Port of Spain [the capital of Trinidad and Tobago] on the night before. Mohan Deora's team, my family, and all the musicians decided to host a lavish birthday lunch for me in what must have been the hotel ballroom or something. Everyone was in a jolly mood. Anil Mohile stood up and announced that he and the musicians wanted to say a few words on the occasion. Anil wished me happy birthday and added, 'Didi has just sung "*Main solah baras ki*" [I am sixteen] for the film *Karz*, and she really still sounds like a sixteen-year-old.' Anil's words were followed by the comments of many musicians. Then the sitarist Jairam Acharya stood up and cheerfully said, 'Didi is so extraordinary that I request all of you to observe a two-minute silence.' For a moment, no one knew how to react and then we all burst out laughing. We just could not stop. Tears of laughter poured down our faces. Poor Jairam had no idea what he had just said. He looked around the room with a confused expression while we could not stop laughing. These small incidents make up a lifetime.

Mumbai, 4 April 2016   LATA MANGESHKAR

Translated by
Nasreen Munni Kabir

1

It Started with a Phone Call

At about 9.55 p.m. on 28 September 1974, the phone rang in my two-bedroom condo in Birmingham, Michigan, a suburb 20 miles from Detroit. My wife, Suvarna, our two children, Aparna and Sunit, and I had lived in Birmingham since 1973. It was late at night, and as people in America do not usually call after 9 p.m., unless there's an emergency, I picked up the phone somewhat fearfully – who could be calling at this late hour? Before I could say 'Hello', the voice on the other end said in an excited tone, 'Mohan, can you guess who this is? Nandi Duggal. I'm calling you from India. I have great news for you. You may not believe it, but I am bringing Lata Mangeshkar for a concert tour to the USA and Canada.'

He went onto ask if I would like to be the national organizer. A national organizer is someone who looks after the whole tour and sells individual shows to organizers/promoters operating in different cities. For a moment I could not believe my ears. To imagine that here was an opportunity for me to work on a Lata Mangeshkar tour! This was the same Nandi Duggal with whom I had organized two concerts in Detroit, the Talat Mahmood show in 1968 and the Kishore Kumar show in 1972. I was aware that Mr Duggal was known for bringing top Indian singers to the US, so his news sounded plausible. A few minutes later, when I had composed my thoughts, I asked, 'What did you say? You're bringing Lata Mangeshkar to the US and Canada?'

'Yes, she'll come with her musicians.'

We spoke some more and discussed a fee of $3,000 for each concert in a nine-city tour. This fee excluded travel and hotel expenses for the group of ten to fifteen people.

I was still in a daze when I put the phone down. The only thing in my mind was the name 'Lata Mangeshkar'. I was one of her umpteen admirers. The first time I had heard her voice was when I was about eight years old and living with my grandparents in Dibrugarh, Assam. In that small town (at least it was a small town when I was growing up), there was a cinema hall with loudspeakers blaring out onto the street. One day my grandmother and I happened to be walking past the cinema and over those loudspeakers we heard the *Mahal* song '*Aayega aanewala*'. It was such a long time ago, but that exquisite voice stayed in my mind. Years later, when I was studying science at Wilson College in Mumbai, a group of students and I were responsible for organizing variety shows that revolved around Hindi film music. By then the songs of Mukeshji and Lataji had come to obsess me and I found planning those shows most satisfying. Perhaps the passion to be involved with a musical tour started back then.

That September night when Nandi Duggal called me in Birmingham, '*Ajaa re ab mera dil pukaara*', '*Barsaat mein hum se mile tum*' and '*Raja ki aayegi baaraat*' played in my mind. In my college days I used to dream that I would somehow produce a Lata Mangeshkar stage show one day and that the orchestra would be led by Shankar–Jaikishan. Could this actually be happening? Not in India, but here in the US where I now lived?

After I had spoken to Nandi Duggal, the next thing I did was to call my concert tour partner Ramesh Shishu. I had to share this incredible news with him no matter how late at night it was. Ramesh is a close friend, and together we had organized music programmes in the past. As I started to tell Ramesh what Nandi Duggal had said, the excitement made me almost breathless. Ramesh asked calmly if I had heard right. Lataji? In America? I assured him that I had not conjured up the story. This was the kind of impact the very thought that she might come to America had on us.

Six days later, Mr Duggal rang back to say that Lataji had decided to postpone the tour and as soon as she gave him the new dates, he would send me the contract. He said the tour would happen for sure and I should just be patient. I was worried. My partner Ramesh's reaction was much the same as mine – he was worried too. But we agreed that there was nothing we could do but wait.

The following week seemed like an eternity and still there was no call. Our patience ran out, so we called Mr Duggal in Mumbai. He had no news for us. The message was clear – something had gone very wrong. Ramesh and I sensed that we had better find another solution and quickly. Then I thought of Mukeshji. During his North American concert tour in 1973, a tour that we had organized, we had become close friends, almost like brothers. Just before Mukeshji boarded the flight to India, he asked me to come and visit him in Mumbai. He added that I should not hesitate to call him if there was anything that he could do for us. During his stay in the US, we talked to him about our dream of bringing Lataji to America on tour, and as Mukeshji was very close to her, he said light-heartedly, 'That's not a big deal. I'll ask her when I return home.'

In this moment of crisis, I thought it would be a good idea to call Mukeshji. The first thing he asked me was whether Lataji had made a commitment to Mr Duggal. I said no. Mukeshji was such an honourable man that he must have thought if Lataji had already come to some agreement with Nandi Duggal, he should not interfere at all. Mukeshji was always transparent in his dealings and here was another proof of it. When he heard that nothing had been settled, he said he would see what he could do. He promised to call back. Then the wait began again.

Some weeks later, Mukeshji called and said I should come to India and meet Lataji personally. I was over the moon. So just before Christmas of 1974, I flew out to Mumbai. The very next day I went to see Mukeshji at his home, 702 Jyoti, on Nepean Sea Road. He greeted me warmly and said he was confident that Lataji would agree, and promised to arrange a meeting.

I was staying with my parents in Malad, but they did not have a phone. Getting a telephone in India of the 1970s was near-impossible, and so I had no choice but to sit for hours at a friend's office, waiting for Mukeshji's call. It seemed as though I had waited for days when finally on 17 December 1974, around ten in the morning, that wonderful phone rang, 'Mohanji, I have talked to Lataji. She has agreed to meet you at Famous Recording Studio in Tardeo tomorrow at 2 p.m.' My heart stopped. The idea of meeting Lata Mangeshkar in person was so overwhelming and kind of nerve-racking too. Her voice had entered my heart, and in many ways I felt I already knew her, but that was so far from the reality.

The next day I arrived at Mukeshji's house around noon. I was very early but I think he understood my impatience to meet her. Together we drove in his car to Famous in Tardeo. Thousands of memorable songs had been recorded there by generations of great composers. It was known to be a lucky studio and a particular favourite of Shankar–Jaikishan. In some interviews, Lataji has talked about recording many Raj Kapoor songs at Famous.

I was both tense and happy when we entered Famous. And there was Lataji. She was sitting on a sofa, wearing a simple, white cotton sari with a green border. For me it was as though I was entering a temple and seeing a vision of Goddess Saraswati.

Mukeshji introduced us, 'This is Mohan Deora. He is the man who organized my American shows.'

I was tongue-tied, and managed to just about whisper, 'Namaste.' Awkwardly, I handed her a bottle of Chanel no. 5. I had heard that she loved French perfumes and could not think of anything else that I could possibly give her. On that day too there was a light fragrance about her. She asked me what I did in America and I explained that I was a nuclear scientist, working for Detroit Edison at their Fermi-2

Nuclear Power Plant. Lataji did not say very much and suggested that Mukeshji bring me to her house the next evening. As I made my way home to Malad, the image of Lataji in her white sari, her soft and sweet voice and gentle smile did not leave my mind.

If you ever happen to drive past Prabhu Kunj on Peddar Road in a taxi, and if the driver is the chatty type, he will probably point to a multi-storey building just as you enter Peddar Road and say that's where Lata Mangeshkar lives. In Mumbai nearly everyone knows that Prabhu Kunj is home to the Mangeshkars. Lataji has a four-bedroom apartment on the first floor and the other flat on the same landing belongs to Asha Bhosle. The Mangeshkars have lived at Prabhu Kunj since the 1960s when they moved there from their home in Walkeshwar.

As agreed, the next day (19 December 1974), Mukeshji and I entered her apartment at Prabhu Kunj. I left my shoes at the entrance, and we made our way in. To our left, I noticed a room that served as a temple, a place of prayer. We were asked to wait in the living room. A few minutes later, Lataji came out of her room and greeted us. Her very first comment to me was, 'So I hear P.L. Santoshi is your father-in-law. *Santoshi Saab ne to mujh se bahut saare gaane gawaayen aur woh ek badey aadmi hain. Woh to mujhe apni picture mein music director banaana chaahte the.*' (I have sung many songs for Santoshi Saab. He's a great man. He had even wanted me to compose music for one of his films.)

My father-in-law, P.L. Santoshi, was indeed a well-known and accomplished film director. He started his career in the late 1930s as an assistant to Jaddanbai (Nargisji's mother), who was an active film-maker in those days. In fact she was among the very first women directors of Indian cinema. Santoshiji later joined Ranjit Studios as a songwriter, and later wrote screenplays and dialogue at Bombay Talkies. Many of his songs are still remembered today, including the famous '*Mehfil mein jal uthi shamaa*' and '*Aana meri jaan Sunday ke Sunday*'. Santoshiji's first film as director was *Shehnai* in 1947. He continued to make many hit films, including *Sargam, Khidkee* and the wonderful *Barsaat ki Raat*. He had also received a gold medal from Dr Rajendra Prasad, the former president of India, for his 1957 film *Hum Panchhi Ek Daal Ke*. My wife, Suvarna, remembers hardly ever seeing her father in her childhood. Santoshi Saab was forever occupied in making movies. She told me what a generous and kind man he was, and if someone ever came to him in need, he would reach into his pockets and without looking at the currency notes he had pulled out, he would hand them over. Lataji made me feel very comfortable by making this family connection.

We then decided to discuss all the details of the tour over dinner, so a few days later we met at the Tanjore Restaurant (renamed Masala Kraft) at the Taj Mahal Hotel. The dinner guests included Mukeshji, Lataji, Khurana Saab (Lataji's accountant) and Raj Singhji, a prince from the royal family of Dungarpur in Rajasthan. Raj Singhji was a famous cricketer and then president of the Cricket Club of India (CCI), i.e., the present-day Board of Control for Cricket in India (BCCI).

Lataji began by saying she was not very keen to perform in America. She said she had no idea how the audience there would react to her. By the end of the evening, Mukeshji, whom she called 'Mukesh Bhaiya', managed to convince her that she must perform in the United States and assured her that everyone would go crazy to see her. To my great relief, she finally agreed.

We settled on a nine-city tour of the USA and Canada. We decided that the shows would be purely musical events and not include comic acts or dance numbers. What took me by surprise was just how well Lataji knew about the style and format of the Indian shows that had been held so far in the West. Even shows with great singers like Mohammed Rafi, Talat Mahmood, Kishore Kumar and Mukesh would feature comic acts and dancers – their shows were more like variety performances.

Over dinner we discussed a fee of $8,000 per show – this included the fees for Mukeshji and the musicians. Lataji is a most perceptive person and she could read a certain apprehension on my face when the issue of money came up – the amount was nearly three times higher than the fees agreed with Nandi Duggal. She said politely, 'I know the cost of the shows has increased a lot. If you feel you'll lose money, do not organize them. I am sure you have already spent a lot of money, so if we do go ahead, you can be the local organizer for Detroit and make the money back.' I was touched by her concern that I might lose money. I reassured her, 'Lataji, your shows are priceless for us and the fees we have agreed upon is fine.'

As we were leaving the restaurant, I shall never forget Mukeshji's parting words to me, 'Mohanji, Lata Mangeshkar *gulaab ke phool ki tarah hain, dhyaan rakhiyega kahin murjhaane ka mauqa na dena, woh badi naazuk hain aur meri toh Didi hain, aur mujhe Mukesh Bhaiya kehti hain.'* (Lata Mangeshkar is a like a rose, be mindful that you do not let the flower wither. She is a sensitive person. She is my sister after all and considers me to be her brother.)

A few days later I had Christmas lunch with Raj Singhji at the Taj. It was most cordial and enlightening. It was there that I got to know the extent of his love for cricket. I also discovered some of Lataji's likes and dislikes. Interestingly, Raj Singhji told me why the deal with Nandi Duggal had finally fallen through. Apparently, Mr Duggal had left an audio recording of one of his shows with her, and Nandi Duggal happened to sing at that show. Lataji listened to the tape and realized this was clearly not a pure musical concert, but an all-round entertainment show. That was not the kind of concert she had in mind, and so she stopped all further discussions with Mr Duggal.

I returned to the US very pleased with the outcome of the Mumbai visit. My partner Ramesh Shishu and I eagerly awaited a signed contract. But nothing came. Out of anxiety we called Mukeshji again and asked him the reason for the delay. He said things were getting complicated. As word got out that Lataji was coming to the States, several people had approached her wanting to organize her tours. We knew we had to go back to India to sort things out.

It was Ramesh's turn this time. I had my day job and taking time off was not always possible. So in early March 1975, Ramesh left for Mumbai where he met Mukeshji who immediately hinted that the financial questions had to be revisited and necessary changes made. Ramesh met Lataji who in turn directed him to Mr Khurana, her accountant. We were very worried that the new terms would make the tour beyond our reach.

Ramesh was informed that instead of an $8,000 fixed fee for each show, Lataji had decided we should have a profit-sharing agreement. Under the terms of this new contract, the net profit would be split 80:20 – 80 per cent for Lataji and 20 per cent for us, with a minimum guarantee of $8,000 per show. Mr Khurana indicated to Ramesh that Lataji had agreed only because Mukeshji believed that we were honest people, and the fact that she had met me personally seemed to help. Three months after our initial discussions, a contract between Lataji and the Image of India (the company we set up for the Lata–Mukesh shows) was signed on 11 March 1975. I remember it was Maha Shivratri, an auspicious day. Mukeshji signed his name as witness.

That contract was the first of many contracts. It broadly outlined these points: Nine shows to be held in the United States and Canada in May 1975 or thereabouts. Our responsibility as national organizers included booking auditoriums, publicity, arranging local orchestras, booking rehearsal rooms, hotels, travel arrangements, getting health insurance cover, and accounting, etc. Principal artist: Lata Mangeshkar accompanied by other senior and junior artists, preferably Shri Mukesh, Usha Mangeshkar, Meena Khadikar (Lataji's younger sister), Anand Bhosle (nephew), Rachana Khadikar (niece, now Shah), Yogesh Khadikar (nephew), conductor/arranger Anil Mohile and various other musicians.

Despite the signed agreement, the local organizers in the US and Canada insisted that we also get a consent letter from Lataji. She immediately instructed Mr Khurana to have the letter typed up, signed by her and handed over. With the agreement and the consent letter in hand, Ramesh flew back to America, very happy and very concerned that we do things right.

2

1975: The Prep, the Arrival

As news spread about Lataji's concert, we were inundated by calls from various cities across the United States and Canada. Several organizers wanted to confirm a show in their city. Before we could get down to signing any agreements, we were faced with a number of challenges during the two months of preparation between March and May 1975. We had naively assumed that since the agreement had been signed, the next thing would be for us to book the airline tickets, find a comfortable hotel and make sure Lataji had a royal reception at the airport. But no.

The first of her many requests involved us giving her a list of cities and venues where the shows would take place. Providing her with the names of local organizers and details about their background experience was Lataji's next request. The third request was to give her two lists of fifty songs each – songs that were popular in the US and likewise in Canada. Lataji was sure that the communities in the US and in Canada would have different musical tastes, as she knew that they were made up of people from very different backgrounds, regions and language groups. For example, in Canada there were many Punjabis who, therefore, spoke Punjabi while the States had more Hindi speakers.

But how were we going to prepare those song lists? In 1975, there were no Asian TV channels as there are today that would have enabled us to ask fans to call in with lists of their favourite songs. Thankfully, however, the cities where the tour would take her (Los Angeles, Vancouver, San Francisco, Toronto, Washington DC, Chicago, Detroit and New York) did have local radio stations that hosted Indian programmes on a regular basis. These programmes were aimed at keeping the community informed of social, political and cultural news.

Both Ramesh Shishu and I hosted a radio show for South Asians in Detroit and we asked our listeners to write in, listing their favourites. That's how we managed to spread the word in our area. Other radio hosts were asked to do the same. Canadian listeners came up with a preference for music that had a strong Punjabi undercurrent, whereas South Asians in the US preferred old favourites and songs based on classical ragas. These lists were sent to Lataji.

We had to rethink ticket prices as well. Tickets for earlier shows ranged between $2.50 and $3.50. Remember, we are talking of the 1970s! So when it came to Lataji's tour, tickets went on sale from $5 scaling to $20. Despite this big jump in price, there was a great demand, and organizers in every city managed to sell the shows with ease. When we signed a contract with a local organizer in Chicago and

Washington, we asked for a minimum guarantee of $25,000 per show, and an 80 per cent split of the net profit (20 per cent to the organizer). In New York and Toronto the minimum guarantee was $80,000.

Another thing that concerned Lataji was the concert venues. She wanted a list of the top auditoriums and to know what kind of sound systems they had, plus details of the stage itself. No one had ever asked us these questions before. Here too she was introducing a new level of professionalism. At first her questions seemed challenging, but actually they helped us to think of the Lata Mangeshkar tour as special – the first of its kind in the US and Canada.

So we sent Lataji a list of venues that included Carnegie Hall in New York, Shrine Auditorium in Los Angeles, John F. Kennedy Center in Washington DC and the O'Keefe Center in Toronto. Booking shows in venues like these was entirely new territory for us. It must be said that the earlier Indian performances were not very well organized or well presented. We used to make do in community halls, schools and colleges. But Lataji had performed to a full house in London's Royal Albert Hall in 1974, and suggesting a community hall was not on the cards. We also came to appreciate that she did not want to make any sort of compromise for the performers or for the audience. She has high standards and taught us how to pay attention to every detail.

The final schedule of the 1975 tour looked like this:

- Friday, 9 May, Shrine Auditorium, Los Angeles
- Saturday, 10 May, Pacific Coliseum, Vancouver
- Sunday, 11 May, Oakland Auditorium Arena, San Francisco
- Saturday, 17 May, Maple Leaf Gardens, Toronto
- Monday, 19 May, Kennedy Center for the Performing Arts, Washington DC
- Friday, 23 May, Civic Opera Hall, San Francisco

- Saturday, 24 May, Ford Auditorium, Detroit (Ramesh and I were responsible for this particular show)
- Sunday, 25 May, Felt Forum at Madison Square Garden
- Monday, 26 May, Carnegie Hall, New York

From the mid-1950s, top classical musicians from India, such as Ravi Shankar or Ali Akbar Khan, were known to have performed regularly in all kinds of mainstream venues in the West. But Lata Mangeshkar was the first singer of Indian film music to perform in these illustrious spaces. She would sing on a stage on which the most famous world musicians had appeared.

These stages have their own incredible history. Take, for example, Detroit's Ford Auditorium. Financed by the Ford Motor Company, the auditorium opened its doors in 1956 (it was demolished in 2011). In its heyday, the Ford Auditorium hosted major pop concerts and theatre plays; even Martin Luther King gave many speeches there.

The Shrine Auditorium, on the other hand, was a very important venue for Hollywood and the music industry – the Oscars took place there ten times. The Shrine hosted several other award ceremonies, including the Screen Actors Guild Award and the Grammys. The Felt Forum in Madison Square Garden (now known as 'The Theatre at MSG') is a high-profile concert venue. Elvis Presley had four shows at MSG in 1972, only three years before Lataji sang there. Countless top jazz musicians and very famous bands played at the famous Carnegie Hall, too many to mention here.

That said, the venues did not come cheap. Rental charges were extremely high. And we soon discovered that no ethnic group had ever approached the management before. What do I mean by 'ethnic group'? In other words – people from India. Our excitement was quickly deflated by the doubting expression on the faces of the managers of these mainly white-run establishments. They had never heard of Lata Mangeshkar, nor could they pronounce her name.

The Ford Auditorium manager asked me, 'Who is this Laatta Maangesker? Do you realize what you're asking? You may not be able to collect enough revenue to pay the basic rent. A month ago a show was booked by a group of Christians from the Middle East – they could not even pay the rent.'

I sat quietly, not sure if I should feel offended. To imagine the manager did not have the slightest idea who Lata Mangeshkar was when millions of people from the Indian subcontinent worshipped her. I suppose I had forgotten that our culture was seen as marginal in the 1970s America. All I could tell the venue manager was, 'Just wait for the tickets to go on sale and watch how quickly they'll disappear. You guys will be bombarded by calls from disappointed and desperate fans.' My confident statement did not reassure anyone, but I think the hefty deposit we left did.

We had another strange experience at the Felt Forum in New York. The managers there imposed a condition on us. Normally, the venue management printed tickets as per their seating plan and then handed them over to the organizers to sell. When it came to our shows it was decided that the management would only give us tickets in small batches. Our organizers would have to sell them, give the money over to the management and then get a fresh batch. We had to follow these rules, but when a significant sum was collected, the management could see that we had a sellout show on our hands. They were astonished and asked us the same question, but this time the tone had changed, 'Who did you say Lata Mangeshkar was?'

The reaction of the Maple Leaf Gardens management in Toronto, where Bob Dylan and Queen had performed, or the John F. Kennedy Center in Washington DC, was much the same. It went on and on. Today, Indian cinema has a greater profile, as the population of Indians, Pakistanis and Bangladeshis have grown and prospered in the West. Indian films and film personalities are also increasingly familiar – at least in some quarters. In the 1970s, people from the Indian subcontinent who lived in the West adored Lata Mangeshkar, but Americans and Canadians were yet to discover what she meant to us.

Communicating with Lataji was another great challenge during the prep months. That was an adventure in itself. We're talking about an era before mobiles and broadband. Given the enormous time difference between the US and India, I would have to telephone her before noon. She had a direct line that would ring in her room at Prabhu Kunj. She would pick up the phone herself and we would have long discussions about the tour preparations. We had quite a time convincing her that she should perform at the Maple Leaf Gardens in Toronto, and not at the O'Keefe Center. Her close friend Nalini Mhatre who lived in Kingston, Canada, advised Lataji to go for the O'Keefe. We explained that the seating capacity at Maple Leaf Gardens was 14,000-plus, as opposed to 3,000 at the O'Keefe Center. Lataji finally gave in.

News that Lata Mangeshkar was coming spread like wildfire. Nothing beats word of mouth in our communities – it is superbly efficient. This was big news for us, and for many it was a childhood dream come true. We must remember that connecting to the homeland in those days was not as easy as it is today. Flights from America to India were expensive and telephone conversation was not cheap either. Hindi films and film songs were a hugely important link for us. And so when Lataji was on her way to perform in our cities for the first time, how could we be anything but keyed up? *Time* magazine had described her as, 'The undisputed and indispensable queen of India's playback singing' – she was that and much more to us. In addition, Lata Mangeshkar was coming with Mukeshji. He was also loved for his wonderful voice, and especially popular were the songs that he sang for Raj Kapoor. We knew the Lata–Mukesh tour of 1975 would be a historic event.

Ramesh and I landed in Los Angeles a week ahead of the team's arrival from India.

We checked into the LA Hilton where we were going to stay. Minute details such as receiving her at the airport, transportation, meal arrangements, backstage refreshments and even the seating positions of each musician on the stage was discussed and decided – this information came from Lataji herself.

Gurudayal Mann, the LA organizer, was overjoyed and confident that he had a sellout show in spite of the ticket price being four times higher than usual. Lataji's sisters, Usha and Meena, and Meena's children, Yogesh and Rachana, and Asha Bhosle's son Anand, were coming too.

They decided to take the Japan Airlines (JAL) flight from Mumbai via Hong Kong, Tokyo and Honolulu. Arrival time in Los Angeles was scheduled for 2 p.m. on 2 May 1975. We headed to the airport well ahead of time to ensure that everything would go smoothly. As soon as we got to the airport, we met the JAL airport manager. We told him just how important Lataji was, and so he made sure that the staff at the VIP lounge would give her a warm welcome. In her typically humble manner, Lataji had requested that her arrival not be announced to the press, to avoid crowds at the airport. Our families were the only people present.

The flight landed and Lataji came through the gates. As she walked towards us, we could hear the subtle tinkling sound of her payal. My six-year-old daughter, Aparna, and Ramesh Shishu's seven-year-old son, Mitul, presented her with a bouquet of flowers.

An hour or so later, we checked into the Hilton, and Lataji's family members made their way to their rooms. The minute Lataji had entered her suite (I still recall the suite numbers 702–704) and before she had time to settle, the phone started ringing and it continued ringing for the next few hours. The calls were from various organizers in the cities where she was going to perform. Her fans were keen to hear her voice, and so she recorded a few sound bites over the phone despite her fatigue.

Lataji had seven days to prepare from the date of her arrival to the first day of the concert on 9 May. Unlike most artists whom we hosted earlier, she was not keen on shopping or sightseeing. She remained occupied with the preparations. Nearly every morning we would go to her room and discuss the shows. I still remember the sweet scent of incense in the room. I learned later that she prayed every morning before the workday would start.

A few days after she had landed, Mukeshji, accompanied by his daughter Nalini (Neelu), and the musicians arrived. On the evening of 7 May, Lataji asked her musicians to assemble the next day in her suite for a rehearsal. I wondered, 'Why a rehearsal?' Never before had any Indian artist suggested rehearsing before a show. So arrangements were made to send the musical instruments to Lataji's suite, and around eleven the next morning, Ramesh and I headed there, knowing that she was very punctual. When we got to her suite, we found the musicians with their sheet music, all ready to start. Lataji was wearing a pastel green sari, and looked relaxed. I had a camera with me, but felt awkward about taking pictures. She immediately put me at ease and said, 'You can take photographs if you like.' I was so touched that I could barely thank her.

A list of twenty-two songs written by our extraordinary composers and lyricists of Hindi cinema was drawn up. The list initially included 'Main to prem deewani' and 'Suno chhoti si gudiya ki lambi kahaani'. But 'Main to prem deewani' had a flute section by Pannalal Ghosh, and Ali Akbar Khan had played the sarod in 'Suno chhoti si gudiya ki lambi kahaani'. Lataji decided to drop these songs from the list, as she felt that these would not sound the same without the presence of these maestros, for whom she had the utmost regard.

Excellent sound quality is the heart and soul of a concert. So she brought Mr Shashank Lalchand with her from Mumbai. Live sound engineers in America are very skilled, but as they may not have been familiar with Indian music and know how to balance the sound of the various Indian instruments on stage, we thought it advisable to have a sound technician from India. Mr Doshi worked out the position of the microphones and monitors on stage. He ended up supervising most of the technical requirements as well.

We had decided that the show would start with Lataji singing a shloka, followed by four songs. Anyone who had worked with Lataji in the Indian film industry knew that she was always on time. She was known to be a stickler for punctuality. That's excellent, but it caused us serious concern. We all know the saying that 'Indians are always late,' and it is close to the truth, and most definitely extends to Indian shows – they would never start on time. On top of that, the audience was complicit in delaying matters further, as they would often roll in half an hour late.

But we had decided to start on time, so latecomers risked entirely missing the first segment, and at the same time disturbing the performer and those who might already be in their seats. To try and avoid such disruptions, we ran an aggressive radio campaign endlessly repeating that Lataji's shows would indeed start as advertised.

Two hours before the curtain call, the musicians arrived at LA's Shrine Auditorium. They were followed an hour later by Lataji and her family and Mukeshji came soon after. She did the final soundcheck herself. When I asked her why she had come so early, she said, 'Mohanji, time is precious and we cannot waste it. My time is as valuable as that of my audience. Many would have travelled miles and miles to get here on time. If we start the show late, I would be wasting the audience's time.'

3

The Big Night in LA

Finally, on Friday, 9 May 1975, the hour of the first Lata–Mukesh concert of the tour had arrived. It was a sellout show at the Shrine Auditorium in Los Angeles. The auditorium is a brilliantly equipped venue and has outstanding acoustics. Many popular bands have played at the Shrine, and in 1975, the popular band Genesis performed there a few months before Lataji. The auditorium is also famous for its Moroccan-style architecture – domes, arches and elaborate filigree. The Shrine has the atmosphere of a Mughal palace.

It was a beautiful spring evening, fragrant with the season's early blossoms. The South Asian community of LA had come out in full force. Fashionably clad, beautifully coiffured women milled around. Men in dark suits, and some wearing Lucknavi kurtas filled the entrance. Six thousand people were ready to stream into that hall. But unlike Western musical concerts where the doors are closed once the performance had started, we knew that such a rule was not practical or imposable on South Asian audiences who were unlikely to accept being shut out. So we had to live with the inevitable latecomers despite our radio campaigns stressing the need for punctuality. The excitement at the Shrine was so great that the people who did come late, and who had to climb over others to get to their seats, went unnoticed. The audience had come to see Lataji and that's all that mattered.

How would she sound? She was so very personal to everyone. She had lent her voice to generations of beautiful screen actresses, and through cinema, radio and television, her songs were deeply embedded in our lives. Our treasured collection of her records was proof of our devotion to her music – those HMV 78 rpm EPs and LPs (music CDs only came into existence in the early 1980s), all stacked proudly in our sitting rooms. And here within a few minutes, Lata Mangeshkar herself would arrive before the impatient crowd.

Since Mukeshji was instrumental in convincing her to come to America in the first place, he believed that introducing her on stage was his responsibility. He spoke with great love and generosity about Lataji. His introduction made the crowds go wild, and the excitement grew more intense when Lataji entered the auditorium. She took off her chappals, and in a gesture of respect touched the podium before she climbed the steps onto the stage itself. Dressed in a simple white sari with a purple border, barefooted, she walked to the microphone, holding some loose papers. On those white sheets of paper, she had written the song lyrics in her own hand. When she stood in front of her music stand, she bowed her head and smiled welcomingly. The six-thousand-strong audience rose to its feet and the auditorium resounded with deafening applause.

When the clapping died down, Lataji began with a shloka from the Bhagavadgita. The verse filled the air. The sweet melody of the shloka was composed by her brother Hridaynath. Then the first musical note of '*Allah tero naam, Ishwar tero naam*' was heard, a noisy round of applause followed. The orchestra conducted by Anil Mohile was made up of only five musicians but they were just brilliant. Arun Paudwal played the accordion; Ramakant Mhapsekar, the tabla; Ravi Kandivali, the mandolin; Rajendra Singh, the swarleen; and Suryanarayan Naidu, the tabla and dholak. Accompanying Lataji and Mukeshji were Usha Mangeshkar, Meena Khadikar, niece Rachana and nephew Yogesh. She sang ten solos and hearing her songs made many in the audience teary-eyed.

My tour partner Ramesh Shishu was also the master of ceremony for the opening show (and for the eight concerts that followed) and when he invited Mukeshji on stage, the audience was ecstatic. They got completely carried away when Mukeshji sang '*Mera joota hai Japani*', '*Ansoo bhari hain ye jeevan ki raahen*', '*Jaane kahaan gaye woh din*' and the unforgettable '*Dil jalta hai to jalne de*'.

Then came the Lata and Mukesh duets – the new and old favourites. It is hard for me to describe the emotion in that arena. There was a hush when they sang '*Aaja re ab mera dil pukara*'. The audience burst out laughing when Mukeshji tried to teach Lataji how to pronounce the word 'sor' in the '*Saawan ka mahina*' song. Usha Mangeshkar sang some beautiful solos, including her chartbuster hit '*Jai jai Santoshi Maata, jai jai ma*'. The two sisters sang '*Gore gore o banke chhore*' together. Lataji invited her sister Meena with her daughter Rachana and son Yogesh to sing the classic *Mother India* song '*Duniya mein hum aayen hain to jeena hi padega*' with her. The concert ended with two numbers: '*Aaja re pardesi*' from *Madhumati* and

Mahal's immortal '*Aayega aanewala*'. Lataji and Mukeshji had successfully kept the audience captive for three-and-a-half hours. What a way to start the tour!

For the second show of the 1975 tour, we landed in Vancouver on 10 May. Vancouver was home to one of the largest Indian populations in North America (mostly Sikhs and Punjabis). The 12,000-seater at the Pacific Coliseum – this is where Tom Jones had performed not long before Lataji – was sold out. Midway through the evening, while she was singing a 'heer' by Waris Shah, the celebrated Punjabi Sufi poet, the one that was used in the film *Heer Ranjha*, someone shouted rudely from somewhere in the upper balcony. This loud and aggressive voice shattered the trance that had engulfed the audience. I could tell that Lataji was visibly upset by the incident. For a sensitive artist it is hard to experience unruly behaviour. It disrupted the sanctity of the moment for Lataji. Yet she continued and gracefully finished singing. The audience gave her a standing ovation and refused to let her leave the stage. Despite that moment of tension, I think the audience took home a once-in-a-lifetime experience.

Once the show was over, we all headed back to the hotel. Lataji preferred to have her dinner in her suite with her family. Normally, after a successful concert, one imagines the artists would enjoy a lively outing at a restaurant with friends, but this was not for Lataji. Over dinner in her hotel suite, the family gathered to discuss her performance and the audience reaction. The applause that each song received suggested to the Mangeshkars the songs that were particularly appreciated. Three of the strongest opinions came from Raj Singh Dungarpur, Bal sahib (Hridaynath) and Ushaji. Following their discussions, the song order was rearranged for the next concert.

It made me wonder why an artist like Lata Mangeshkar needed a critical appraisal of her performance. All her songs were met by loud applause and many standing ovations; so what was the point of rearranging the song order? Or for that matter changing the song selection? I suppose the answer lay in the fact that Lata Mangeshkar strives for perfection, to keep improving, raising standards, to sing as perfectly as humanly possible. It made me think of Bade Ghulam Ali Khan's famous comment, *'Kambakht, kabhi besura nahin gaati'* (The wretched girl never sings a note out of tune.)

The response to her shows was the same in every venue and in every city. At San Francisco's Oakland Coliseum *'Thandi hawaayen'*, *'Mohe bhool gaye sanwaria'*, *'Inhi logon ne'*, *'Barsaat mein'* and some new numbers received rapturous applause. In his unique style, Mukeshji brought the Raj Kapoor numbers alive, including *'Awaara hoon'*, *'Mera joota hai Japani'* and *'Honton pe sachaaii rehti hai'*. Memories of India, bitter-sweet days of childhood, dreams of youth all came rushing back.

What stayed in my mind from that San Francisco trip was our visit to Fisherman's Wharf. Lataji was reluctant to play tourist, but her nephews and niece insisted. So we ended up having a lovely outing and a fabulous meal at a seafood restaurant at Fisherman's Wharf. I discovered that Lataji loved seafood, especially anything hot and spicy. It was wonderful to hear her laugh and enjoy an experience of America.

It was probably the long lines of people waiting to buy tickets for the Lata Mangeshkar concerts that attracted the attention of the American press, including *The Washington D.C. Post* and *The Christian Science Monitor*. Journalists from these newspapers came to ask for information about her. Their articles had headlines like 'Lata, the Lady in white wins America', 'A legend from India wins America' and 'Ghost Nightingale'. The ghost nightingale title was intended to liken the role of a playback singer, who lends her voice to an actress, to that of a ghostwriter.

When we were in Washington, Lataji and the team stayed at the famous Watergate Hotel. The next day, she asked to visit the Arlington National Cemetery where John F. Kennedy is buried. The Mangeshkars also visited other historical places including the White House and the Smithsonian Institution.

At Toronto's Maple Leaf Gardens show on 17 May, the manager, who had seriously doubted our ability to sell enough tickets to cover the rent for the 14,000-seater, shook my hand during the interval and said excitedly, 'Congratulations, sir! Your revenue has crossed $100,000. That's even higher than the sum Frank Sinatra earned when he performed here recently.'

A very famous journalist and commentator, Gordon Sinclair, talked at length about Lata Mangeshkar on his radio show. Several newspapers that rarely printed anything on Indian music, beyond articles on Ravi Shankar's concerts, covered the Toronto show. *The Toronto Sun* (May 1975) went into great and amusing detail about Lataji and Indian cinema: 'Lata Mangeshkar is what is known as a "playback singer". That is the vocalist who replaces the voice of the leading lady whenever she breaks into song. In Indian movies the leading lady does so with astonishing regularity. Mile for mile, India is reported to be the world's leading commercial film producer, but almost all of that country's movies fit a formula far more strict than ever our Westerns were. Almost all of them are family dramas with conflict patterns similar to *Romeo and Juliet*. The lovers have to overcome the hurdles of their difference in class or religion before they find fulfillment ... In the interim, the heroine almost always gets to knock off six or seven songs. And most of the time – if the actress is anyone important – her singing voice is supplied by Lata Mangeshkar ... another obstacle for the potential fan from the media-saturated Western world is the show's rigorous lack of visual distraction. There is no dance, no interpretive acting – just the music. The music, on this show, then, may well be an acquired taste, but what better chance to try and acquire it.'

Mr and Mrs Raj Kapoor happened to be vacationing in New York and Mukeshji went to see them at their hotel. He requested Raj

Saab to make an appearance at the Felt Forum show and he kindly agreed. On 25 May 1975, Mukeshji started the evening by requesting the showman of Indian cinema to introduce Lataji. The audience went wild with delight to see the legendary Raj Kapoor step onto the stage. He had to wait a long time before the applause died down. He started by saying that he was pleased to see so many Indians in a foreign land, a land across the seven seas (saat samundar), as he put it. He then spoke with great affection about Lata Mangeshkar: 'She has been blessed by Goddess Saraswati. I am lucky that I work in the same era as her. I know "*Kal khel mein hum hon na hon*" (Tomorrow I may no longer be a player in life's game), but I pray that Lataji's voice will continue echoing for hundreds of centuries. It will remind us all that "*Hum us desh ke waasi hain jis desh mein Ganga behti hai*" (We are from the land where the Ganga flows).' He also added, 'When people in Russia sing '*Awaara hoon*' they think of Raj Kapoor, but it is really Mukesh Chand.' He described himself as a flute with holes in its body, and the air that blows through the flute to bring out the sound and music belongs to Mukesh. Raj Saab asked his wife Krishnaji to join him on the stage and present flowers to Lata Mangeshkar. The audience was over the moon. After Lataji had finished the shloka, Mukeshji sang '*Dost dost na raha*', a particular favourite of the New York audience. At the tour finale there were other cinema personalities who attended, including Yash Chopra, Hema Malini, Padmini Kolhapure and the famous Pakistani singer and actress, Musarrat Nazir.

Mukeshji told us the nine-city tour felt like a fairy tale. But the exciting month had to come an end. My partner Ramesh Shishu and I felt sad to say goodbye to Lataji and her team as they boarded the flight to India from the New York airport. We also felt a certain pride in having collaborated in a record-breaking and historic musical event.

4

The Ground Beneath Us Shook

The complaint we later heard about the 1975 tour was that people from smaller cities in the US and Canada were unable to attend the shows because of the distances involved, and as a result, Lataji's fans flooded her with requests to also perform in smaller centres. Dr Sid Mittra and I were the national organizers and so we decided to add other cities to our list, including Montreal, Cleveland, Boston, New Jersey and Milwaukee. Sid was my associate for the 1976 Lata–Mukesh tour and was also the master of ceremony and, as usual, the auditoriums in these cities were identified and the list was sent to Lataji in India.

We were much better prepared this time round and so everything was soon in place. It was decided that Nitin Mukesh would come to America with his father. We kicked off the Lata–Mukesh 1976 tour in Vancouver on 1 August at the Queen Elizabeth Hall. The Vancouver organizer, Sudesh Kalia, made sure we had additional security because of the unpleasant incident that had occurred at the last Vancouver concert involving an unruly spectator. From the very start of the tour, Lataji appeared more relaxed offstage, and on stage. She had the experience of the 1975 shows behind her and the tremendous reaction from the audience showed her just how much she was loved.

My friend Dr Sid Mittra received Lataji at the Vancouver airport and the first question she asked him was whether he was a PhD. Before he could answer, Dr Mittra remembered thinking: 'For a moment I was literally frozen in my tracks. But I soon came back to my senses, and managed to answer her by merely nodding my head.' A fascinating conversation then followed between Sid and Lataji.

'Mittraji,' Lataji said, 'I presume that once you have obtained your PhD, you have earned that title for the rest of your life and never have to take another exam again. Is that right? That's very nice. But imagine, every time I am in front of the microphone, whether in a recording studio or on the stage, I feel I am being asked to pass a PhD exam. Because every song I sing is closely scrutinized by people of all ages and of diverse backgrounds and who speak different languages. That is the constant challenge I face. A challenge that I can never ignore.'

Sid Mittra later told me: 'That brief encounter I had with Lataji, almost four decades ago, answered two critical questions that, I think, have helped to define her place in history and why she has reached the top of the musical world and remained there for several generations. She has set the bar so high that it has become virtually impossible for any singer to reach it, let alone cross it.'

There was another incident involving Sid Mittra that I'd like to share in his words: 'It was way past midnight, 2 a.m. to be exact. The place was a recording studio in downtown Detroit, not the safest place in the world by any means. I was standing behind an eight-track recorder, and the sound engineer was busy mixing the pre-recorded tracks to create a final mix. Through the monitor I could hear the last line of the song in which the singer held onto a very high-pitched note.

'Suddenly, the sound engineer, Bob Morris, turned to me, looked at me straight in the eye and asked: "Sid, I don't know anything about Indian instruments, I only know a little about the sitar because of Ravi Shankar, so don't mind my asking you a dumb question. Can you tell me the name of the instrument that is being played on this tape right now?"

'The sound Bob was hearing was not the sound of an Indian instrument – it was not a violin, sarangi, or esraj. It was the voice of Lata Mangeshkar. Bob was flabbergasted when I told him it was a human voice. The mesmerized Bob continued: "I have been a sound engineer for twenty-five years and have recorded the music of many famous performers. But I must honestly confess that I have never – I repeat never – heard this quality of a human voice." He paused for a moment and then added: "If you ever get a chance to meet this gifted singer, please tell her that Bob salutes her.'"

Lataji enthralled the audience at every concert in 1976. At every show we could see thousands of smiling people, the emotion rushing to their hearts when she would sing a familiar song. Outside of a recording studio, people had never witnessed the camaraderie that existed between Lataji and Mukeshji, so this too came as a delightful surprise.

When we realized that Lataji was more relaxed, we suggested that we visit the sights in Vancouver. One day when we were driving around the city, we heard a tinkling sound every time the driver applied his brakes. Lataji was intrigued and asked, '*Ye awaaz kahaan se aa*

rahi hai?' (Where is this sound coming from?)
The driver, a Sardarji, replied in Punjabi, '*Aji
ye bell bandh rakhi hai, gadi chalte samay apne
gaon di yaad dilaati hai ji.*' (I've tied a bell to the
brakes so whenever I brake, I hear a light jingling
sound. It reminds me of a bullock cart making
its way through my village in Punjab.) Lataji
smiled and said, '*Wah, Sardarji, kya baat hai!*'
(Bravo, Sardarji. That's wonderful!)

We had four days off before the second
concert of the tour at the PAC Auditorium in
Milwaukee; so Mukeshji suggested that we fly to
Las Vegas for a short break. Since the idea had
come from Mukeshji, her loving brother, how
could Lataji refuse? The word filtered down to
the whole team and everyone got very excited
to see Las Vegas, the world's gambling capital.
Some people even call it 'the city of lost wages'.

We checked into the Las Vegas Hilton and,
as we were walking towards the elevators, we
could hear the sound of coins dropping from a
slot machine. Lataji was soon taken by the slot
machines. She thoroughly enjoyed playing them

and was delighted when she won and could see the coins tumbling out. This trip turned out to be so relaxing for us all. What I did not know then was that our journey to Las Vegas would be the first of many. Whenever we had any free time, we would head there. Rumour quickly spread in India that Lataji enjoyed gambling in Las Vegas!

We performed in Milwaukee, Washington DC, Houston, Cleveland, Boston, Montreal and Toronto. Covering the Boston show, the music critic Richard Dyer at *The Boston Globe* (23 August 1976) wrote: 'There were lengthy introductions of impeccable courtesy before Lata Mangeshkar came out before the microphone. A small woman, clad in a white sari, Mangeshkar avoids any show-biz effects. She simply stands in front of her music rack, adjusts her glasses, marks time with her left hand and starts to sing ... He [Mukesh] is a very attractive performer with a soft-edged, even fuzzy voice, rather like Bing Crosby's, though one with great technical resilience.'

Seven cities later, we landed in Detroit, my home territory, two days before the 27 August show at the Ford Auditorium. We checked into the Hotel Pontchartrain (Lataji called it Panchatantra), and the musicians and artists settled in. Mukeshji was in his element and insisted on playing cards all afternoon at the hotel with the musicians.

The next evening (26 August), I invited them for an informal dinner at home. I drove Mukeshji and Lataji 20 miles from Detroit to my place in Birmingham. Mukeshji used to enjoy a glass of scotch before dinner, but never after dinner. However, he did not drink alcohol in front of Lataji. He once told me that even Raj Kapoor would hesitate to drink in front of her. That was the kind of respect she commanded. However, that evening I was pleasantly surprised to hear Mukeshji courteously ask her if he could have a drink. Lataji immediately said, 'What difference does it make? Go ahead.' I poured him a drink, and he insisted that I have one too. I was embarrassed, 'No, Mukeshji, not in front of Lataji.' She overheard me, turned to me and repeated, 'What difference does it make? Go ahead.' I filled my glass, but couldn't get myself to swallow a single drop.

We had a lovely evening and when we were driving back to the hotel after dinner, Mukeshji said with a big smile, 'The chicken was the best chicken I have ever eaten. And to think it was cooked in the home of a vegetarian!'

The next day, 27 August, was the day of the concert. As usual the show was a sellout. That afternoon I had to meet a friend for lunch and asked Mukeshji to join me. He declined, saying he was engrossed in a card game with the musicians.

Around 5 p.m., Mukeshji was getting ready to leave for the show when suddenly he felt very unwell. His son, Nitin, immediately asked the hotel reception to get an ambulance. The ambulance arrived and rushed him to the Detroit General Hospital. I got a call from the hotel saying Mr Mukesh had had a heart attack and had been rushed to the hospital. The ground beneath me shook. I cried, 'Heart attack?'

I drove furiously to Detroit General, and coincidentally, the song that was playing on the Indian radio channel was '*Dil jalta hai to jalne de*'. I was distraught and ran towards the Emergency Room. Lataji and Nitin were in the waiting area. An eerie silence hung in the air. I saw my friend Dr Balak Verma, whom I called as I left home, coming towards us. It was he who broke the news, 'We tried very hard to revive him, but could not save him. He is no longer with us.'

It seemed so unreal. How could this happen? Mukeshji was so cheerful that very afternoon, laughing and playing cards. We were all in a state of shock, or should I say in a state of denial? How could we accept the devastating news? It was a devastating loss.

In silence, we drove back to the hotel. Lataji sat beside Nitin in the back and held his hand. I felt numb, not knowing what to do. When we got to the hotel, Lataji took me aside and said in a tearful voice, 'Mohan Bhaiya, be brave. Pay all the artists and the local organizer. I don't want anyone to suffer any loss. Don't worry about the money. Tomorrow we will take Mukeshji's body to New York. We will spend the night there and then go back to India. Please go to the auditorium and break the news to the audience.'

I rushed to the Ford Auditorium, which was within walking distance from the hotel, and told Dr Sid Mittra what had happened. We asked Hridaynathji to announce the news to the people of Detroit, and apologize about our having to cancel the show. The local organizer in Philadelphia, where we were supposed to go next, called us. He insisted that the show must go on, but for everyone, particularly Lataji, losing Mukeshji was a terrible trauma, and she was in no state to perform.

When I returned to Lataji's suite, I could hear the constant ringing of the telephone. People were calling from all over America and India. Before I could say anything, Lataji said in quiet voice, 'Mohan Bhaiya, *main ye khabar Bhabhiji ko kaise doon? Mujh mein himmat hi nahin hai.*' (Mohan Bhaiya, how can I break this news to my sister-in-law, Mukeshji's wife? I don't have the courage.) I dialled Mukeshji's home number in Mumbai. The phone rang and someone picked it up. I handed the phone to Lataji and heard her consoling voice. She was broken inside.

I went downstairs to the hotel lobby where my friend Arvind Shah was waiting. I was in tears. He briefed me about what had taken place when Hridaynathji addressed the auditorium. The whole audience rose to their feet in tribute to their beloved Mukeshji. After a two-minute silence, it was announced that the show was cancelled and that the tickets would be refunded. The audience showed such dignity and restraint. One by one they emptied the hall in silence. Some were crying quietly.

Arvind Shah, who owned Jaya and Sky Bird travel agencies (he provided an excellent service for all the travel during Lataji's concerts from 1975 to 1998), guided me through all the formalities. He was of crucial help to me. Before Mukeshji's body could be flown to New York from where the journey to India would begin, arrangements had to be made with a funeral parlour, so that they would take Mukeshji's body from Detroit General Hospital and prepare it. The people at the funeral parlour asked me to get Mukeshji's clothes for them. I went back to Nitin's hotel room and asked him to give me his father's light blue suit, a white shirt and Mukeshji's favourite red tie.

The next morning I woke up early and drove to the funeral parlour to drop off the clothes. They asked me to select a coffin. I could not bear to do it, but I had no choice, I had to. I drove to the hotel and went up to Nitin's room. The door opened. Nitin's eyes were bloodshot from a sleepless and impossibly sad night. I put my hand on his shoulder and he burst into tears. I tried to calm him down and asked if he had eaten anything. He could not speak. I took him down to the coffee shop and insisted that he would have to eat something.

We drove to the funeral parlour after breakfast. The staff was very courteous and led us into a room where the coffin lay. Dressed in his light blue suit, white shirt and red tie,

Mukeshji was lying in the open casket. Even with his eyes closed, I felt a sort of vibration as though he were saying something. I could not control my emotions, and tears rolled down my face. I placed a red rose in the open casket and closed my eyes. We could hear the sound of falling rain through the open window.

We flew from Detroit to New York's JFK airport in the same plane as Mukeshji's body. We landed at JFK and were received by Jayant Parmar who had booked a hotel for us and had made all the necessary arrangements. At the airport, a radio journalist (Lalitaji) asked Lataji for her comments. I was not sure whether this was the right time for an interview and tried to avoid the journalist. But Lataji gave a nod of approval and said, 'I don't know what to say about Mukesh Bhaiya. We came on tour last year and who would have imagined that this tour would end like this. We are shocked and deeply saddened. Mukesh Bhaiya and I go back twenty-five years. Everyone loved him. He was a man of God, a great singer. There are millions of his fans in India, I cannot count how many. Music was his life. I am sure that Nitin will build on his father's legacy. Even when Mukesh Bhaiya was unwell he would sing. He once told his son that he would die singing. He did not wish to die at home, in a comfortable bed. He wanted to go singing. May God bless his soul and give him peace.'

I still remember seeing, through a glass divider, the coffin with Mukeshji's body moving along the conveyer belt towards the cargo area of Air India. It was my last goodbye.

5

Setting the Trend: 1977–80

Following Mukeshji's passing away in 1976, Lataji and I stayed in regular contact. She told me that she had released an album as a tribute to her dear brother. He was always present in our phone conversations. It was during one such conversation that she told me that Mukeshji firmly believed that no work should be left incomplete. And so Lataji felt that we must return to Detroit and Philadelphia to make up for the cancelled concerts. She had heard how the Detroit audience had reacted the night it was announced that Mukeshji had passed away.

The heartfelt respect they showed moved her very much.

In 1977, we tried to organize a show in Detroit, but the winter was very severe that year, so instead we ended up scheduling three concerts elsewhere. One was held at the Felt Forum (MSG) in New York, the second at the Valley Forge in Philadelphia and the third at the Shrine Auditorium in Los Angeles.

Describing the New York show, Robert Palmer of *The New York Times* (17 January 1977) wrote: 'When Westerners think of Indian music, most of them think of the classical style as represented by Ravi Shankar or Ali Akbar Khan. But the music one hears in most Indian households, and in most of the city's Indian restaurants, is Indian film music, and the reigning queen of the idiom, Lata Mangeshkar, gave a rare public performance at the Felt Forum ... accompanied by percussion, violin, harmonium, accordion and mandolin, and reading her music from a stand, she sang in a remarkable voice that was very high yet very substantial, with exceptional intonation. Her listeners, most of whom had heard her in countless films but had never seen her perform, seemed enraptured.'

The Shrine event was in fact a charity concert for the Hare Krishna Society. And so we were housed in an apartment complex where Hare Krishna devotees lived. It was quite an experience to live in that spiritual environment. It almost felt as though we were living inside a temple. Every morning and evening we could hear the ringing of bells and the sound of praying. We had a very peaceful time there. In an interview, Lataji expressed her love for Lord Krishna and said how much she liked the Hare Krishna Society.

The charity show itself, held on Sunday, 30 January, was a fine mix of American and Indian culture. Lataji sang to an enchanted audience. A senior member of the Hare Krishna Society spoke of her so beautifully when he said that her voice sounded as pure as water falling into a forest pond.

During the intermission, Lataji and her co-singers mingled with the audience with collection baskets, asking for donations on behalf of the Hare Krishna Society. I can never forget the sight of Lataji's jholi spread in front of her fans. The proceeds from the show helped towards the building of a large centre called ISKCON in Juhu in Mumbai, which opened a year later, in 1978.

We returned to the apartment complex after the concert, and as Lataji got out of the car, she saw a long line of Krishna devotees waiting to greet her. They played their dholak and manjira (small hand cymbals), and as she walked past, they showered her with rose petals. I was following close behind and I could see that Lataji was very moved.

In 1978, my wife Suvarna travelled to India because her father P.L. Santoshi was taken seriously ill. On 7 September 1978, he passed away at KEM Hospital in Mumbai, aged sixty-two. My mother-in-law, whose birthday fell on 8 September, lamented that her dear husband had left her a day before the celebration. I was in America at the time and unable to join my wife in Mumbai because of work commitments. P.L. Santoshi had been a big name in the Indian film industry but had been facing lean times in the 1970s; it was sad to see that very few film people attended the funeral.

Two years passed before we could organize another tour. On the personal front, my family and I moved into a bigger house in another Detroit suburb called Troy, which was not far from where we earlier lived in Birmingham, Michigan. This was during the first week of March 1979. And finally in 1980, the next tour took us to Washington, Chicago, Detroit, New York and then Toronto.

This time the marvellous Manna Dey was Lataji's co-singer. They had sung so many superb duets together like *'Pyar hua ikraar hua'* and *'Aaja sanam madhur chaandni mein hum'*. They were good friends too. When they arrived in the States, Manna Dey chose to stay with my friend Amit Ghosh. And Lataji said that she and her family would prefer to stay at my house rather than in a hotel. It was a spontaneous decision and we were very happy and privileged to have them stay with us.

A typical day for Lataji would start with her puja and lighting of agarbattis. The fragrance of incense would fill the house. She would come out of her room and the sound of her payal would resonate wherever she went. Lataji's breakfast was hot coffee, English muffins, orange marmalade and honey. Sometimes she had some cornflakes or muesli with cold milk. Lunch was simple: a bowl of broccoli, or chicken noodle soup and toast. Dinner was an Indian meal with daal, rice, roti, chicken curry and vegetables. To my surprise she loved papad and mangodi (mung dal pakoda). She has a sweet tooth and her list of likes were many – gaajar ka halwa, baadaam halwa, ras malai, gulaab jaamun, motichoor ka laddu, etc.

During the week she stayed with us, one particular evening is still etched on my mind. It was dinner time and I could not see Lataji anywhere. I asked Suvarna where she was and she said Lataji might be in the basement. As I walked down to the basement, I could not believe my eyes – she was sitting with my seven-year-old daughter Aparna in her lap. Aparna had a slight fever and Lataji was rubbing her feet. I ran upstairs to my wife and asked her to come and see this heart-warming sight.

On 14 September 1980, we were at the Arie Crown Theater in Chicago for the tour's second show. Just as we were entering the theatre, we saw Richard Burton walking out. He was carrying a puppy in his hands. Lataji was going to perform on the same set that had been built on the stage for *Camelot*, starring Burton. The stage manager came to me and said, 'The set will stay on the stage and Mr Burton's representative will mind the set. Mr Burton has said that you'll have to pay $1,500 for his man's time. He will make sure that nothing is damaged.' I talked to our local organizer and we agreed to pay the fee.

Before the start of the show, and knowing how punctual Lataji was, I became anxious because the stage was not ready for us. Richard Burton's man moved about very slowly and I was getting irritated and impatient. I was forced to tell him, 'Please clear the stage right away, any further delay may cause our show to start late. Unless you guys move, we will sue Mr Burton for delaying our start time.' The message got through and we could at last prepare the stage for our audience.

The show at the Ford Auditorium in Detroit started off on a very sombre note. As usual, Lataji sang a shloka from the Bhagavadgita. She was in a quiet and solemn mood when she addressed the audience, 'Brothers and sisters, four years ago we came to America with Mukesh Bhaiya, and I am sure you will remember the tragedy that befell us when Mukesh Bhaiya left us forever. I will never forget the love and kindness that you, the people of Detroit, showed us. We were in a state of shock and really did not know what to do. When my brother Hridaynath gave you the news, I heard that you all stood up and blessed Mukesh Bhaiya's soul and observed a two-minute silence. I can never forget these things. From that moment, I have felt a special bond with the people of Detroit, and I regard Detroit as my second home. And think of Mohan Deora as my brother. I do not usually sing the songs of other singers, but today, in memory of Mukesh Bhaiya, I shall sing a very moving song of his, '*Jaane kahaan gaye wo din*'.

I could not imagine a more fitting tribute. Lataji put her heart and soul into the singing. I could sense her pain and loss. The audience was moved beyond words. Many were crying and I must admit I could not hold my tears back either.

Lataji kept the audience captivated for the rest of the evening. A highlight for the audience was the semi-classical '*Saawan ke jhoolen padhe*'. Midway through the performance, Lataji addressed the audience again, 'I am sure you know that Nargisji is critically ill and is currently receiving treatment at the Sloan Kettering Hospital in New York. I would like you all to pray that she gets better very soon.' She then sang the beautiful '*Rasik balma*', a song that Nargisji had lip-synched in *Chori Chori*.

A rather awkward incident then took place. While Lataji and Manna Dey were singing '*Jhoomta mausum mast maheena / ya'allah, ya'allah dil le gayi*', a gentleman threw some dollar notes onto the stage. This may have been his way of appreciating the singing, but Lataji was alarmed. She completed the song and said firmly, '*Abhi abhi ek saab stage par kuchh paise phenk kar gayen hain. Mera unse kehna hai ki is tarah paise phenk kar aap hamaara apmaan na karen. Agar aap ko hamaara gaana pasand aaya hai, toh hamein taaliyon se swaagat kar ke humein aashirwaad dijiye, is tarah hamaara apmaan naa karen. Jo sajjan ye paise phenk kar gayen hain, wo aa kar ye paise utha kar le jaayen, please.*' (A gentleman has just thrown some money on the stage. I would like to tell him not to insult us. If you like our singing, please clap and give us your blessings, but do not insult us. I request the gentleman to please come and take his money back.)

Lataji believes strongly that artists must be respected at all times and under all circumstances. This kind of behaviour, even done without malice, was unacceptable to her. The admirable thing about her was how fearless she could be to publicly say what she thought, if she believed an artist was being disrespected. Whether professionally or personally, she continues to show a deep respect for people and treats everyone equally. She does not make anyone feel inferior.

The awkwardness of the moment passed and for the very first time during the tours, Lataji presented a medley in different Indian languages. The audience was made up of people from various regions of the Indian subcontinent and they were touched to hear her sing in their mother tongue. The medley was received with a roar of delight and the applause just went on and on. She ended the evening by thanking her co-singers, her brother Hridaynath and the sound engineer Shashankji.

The surprise guest for the two 1980 shows in New York and Toronto was none other than

Amitabh Bachchan. He flew into New York on a Concorde flight on a Friday, appeared on the stage in New York and Toronto and left on Monday morning.

With a number of blockbusters behind him, by the mid-1970s, Amitabh Bachchan had become the most popular Indian star ever. In his heyday he had no rivals. *India Today* called him the one-man industry and that was an apt description.

I went to JFK airport to receive Amitji and Jayaji and while we were on our way to the hotel, he asked about Nargisji. When he heard that she was at the Sloan Kettering Hospital, he said he wanted to go there. Sunil Duttji greeted us very warmly and led us to Nargisji's room. She was under treatment for cancer. Amitji and Jayaji were most comforting and chatted with her for a short while. As we were coming out of the hospital gate, I saw Lataji's limousine driving in. I waved to her and we carried onto the Waldorf Astoria Hotel.

That very evening Amitabh Bachchan called Lataji and expressed his gratitude for having invited him to be part of her concert. He asked about the schedule and when he learned that Lataji had a rehearsal at the Felt Forum (MSG) at 9 a.m. the next day, Amitji asked if he could come along. At 9 a.m. on the dot, punctual as ever, Amitji arrived and joined in the rehearsals. Lataji encouraged him to perform a song on stage and he agreed. He began by rehearsing a folk song from Uttar Pradesh, '*Mere angne mein tumhaara kya kaam hai*'. This song would eventually find its way into his hit film *Laawaris* a couple of years later.

The New York concert was overbooked and crowds of people clamoured for tickets. Tickets were being sold in the black market for three or four times the original price. To the delight of those South Asians who managed to get seats, this most popular Indian star performed a song and dance for the 6,000-strong audience. At the end of the song, he was greeted with thunderous applause. This might have been one of Amitji's earliest live appearances before an audience of US-based South Asians. The fans went crazy to see their hero in the flesh.

The press loved it too, and many articles followed, including a feature in the September 1980 issue of *India Abroad*. 'Lata Mangeshkar is the biggest name in the world of Indian popular music, cutting across regions and languages. A live concert by her is therefore an important event for her vast following. To add luster to the evening's programme, matinee idol Amitabh Bachchan made a special guest appearance.'

When the show ended, Amitji told Lataji, 'Wow, this is an unforgettable event. Now I know how you must feel when you see your fans cheering for you. Today I have experienced that special feeling. What is there in performing in a movie? Performing for a live audience is something special!'

In those days, there were a limited number of stage shows in India, nor were there hundreds of television and satellite channels that aired countless award ceremony shows with their extravagant song-and-dance numbers. So it was most unusual to see a movie star from India performing live. I am sure our shows must have triggered the idea in Amitabh Bachchan's mind to do the same going ahead.

At the last concert of the tour, on 21 September, there was not a single empty seat in sight at the Maple Leaf Gardens in Toronto, a 14,000-seater. I could see Amitji looking through the wings at the mesmerized faces of the audience. There was palpable energy in the air and all attention was directed to the stage. When Amitabh Bachchan returned to India, he undoubtedly talked to his people about organizing stage shows in America. It did not take him long, and in 1981, he fronted, along with some of his movie heroines, a music-cum-dance show. I remember some senior artistes criticized him for dancing on the stage, saying, '*Hero ho kar stage par dance karta hai?*' (A star, a film hero, dancing on stage?)

Yet who would have expected that Lataji's simple request would start an entirely new dimension to Bollywood show business? And Amitji's shows would draw thousands and thousands of his fans settled outside India, and his song '*Mere angne mein tumhaara kya kaam hai*' would always create a favourite moment in his subsequent shows.

The Amitabh Bachchan shows were followed by shows featuring other top Indian stars, including Shah Rukh Khan, Salman Khan and Akshay Kumar. They now regularly tour America, Canada and Europe. And so, thanks to Lataji, South Asian audiences who have settled in all parts of the world and who do not usually go to Western musicals or rock and pop concerts, can enjoy an evening's entertainment of their choice.

I still remember a small incident involving Amitabh Bachchan from our 1980 experience. As he and I entered the green room, after the evening show at the Felt Forum, a girl who was hiding in the bathroom, jumped out and grabbed hold of him tightly and screamed, 'I love you.' Amitji and I looked at each other, mouths agape.

6

A Promise Fulfilled: 1980–83

Mukeshji would often tell Lataji that one day he would take her to Guyana and the Caribbean islands. *'Wahan ke log aap ki pooja karte hain aur aap ko sun ne ke liye taras rahe hain.'* (People there worship you and long to hear you sing.)

Lataji decided to honour Mukeshji's wish. And so I got working. I made several trips to the West Indies and finally managed to schedule a concert tour in 1980. This time Nitin Mukesh would accompany Lataji. This was the announcement I made: 'Friends, it is with great pleasure that I bring you news of

Miss Mangeshkar's forthcoming tour. India's nightingale, the incredible Lataji, is coming to Guyana. Many individuals have helped in this endeavour, and I am personally grateful to Guyana's government officials who have made the tour possible. Let me assure you that Lataji is looking forward to being here amongst you, and is touched by the love, respect and regard that the Guyanese people hold in their hearts for her.'

All the arrangements were made for our arrival. We were to fly from Toronto to Trinidad. We checked in and got busy shopping duty-free. The boarding had begun and some of our team had boarded the flight, but many, including Lataji and I, failed to hear the final call and the worst happened: we missed the flight.

There was a group of us and by now we were absolutely frantic. Our bags had been checked-in and we had no clothes or personal belongings. We were stranded in Toronto. Somehow we made our way to a nearby motel where we stayed the night. To add to our woes, the next flight to

Trinidad was via New York, and as luck would have it, Lataji's American visa had expired. So, she needed a transit visa.

We made our way to the US consulate in Toronto, hoping we could persuade them to give us a visa, which was not usually an easy task. We filled out the visa application and when we were called in for the personal interview, something amazing happened. The American consul general welcomed us into her office and greeted us with a 'namaste'. I have no words to describe what went through my mind. She then continued addressing me in impeccable Hindi, '*Yeh Lata Mangeshkarji hai na?*' (This is Lata Mangeshkar, isn't she?) I blurted out a yes. '*Inke gaane sun kar maine Hindi sikhi hai, kya mujhe inka autograph mil sakta hai?*' (I have learned Hindi by listening to her songs. Do you think she might give me an autograph?)

What a turn of events. It made me think how little we knew of the widespread, and largely undocumented, impact of Hindi films in those days. Some years later, one heard stories of

Indians making friends with people of vastly different cultures all around the world because of a common love for Hindi films or film songs. Even in the remotest corners of the world, the songs of Lataji, Rafi Saab or Mukeshji have allowed Indian travellers to start a conversation with strangers – and before you knew it, you had made a new friend who, with a big smile on their face, could hum the tune of *'Awaara hoon'* or *'Mera joota hai Japani'.*

The crisis was over. The visa was granted with a warm handshake and we went back to the motel in Toronto. On our way back, Lataji asked me, *'Mohan Bhaiya, wo Amrican lady aap se Hindi mein baat kar rahi thi ya aap English mein hi bole jaa rahe thay?'* (Was the American lady talking to you in Hindi, or were you chatting away with her in English?) I smiled. I still don't have the answer to Lataji's question. Her sharp wit can really be matchless.

Lataji's long-awaited concert was scheduled at 8 p.m., at the Jean Pierre Complex, Port-of-Spain (the capital of Trinidad and Tobago), on

Saturday, 27 September 1980. There were two back-to-back concerts in the same venue, and both shows were sold out weeks in advance. We arrived at the 10,000-seater stadium and were amazed to see there wasn't a single empty seat. I was told that people had come with their picnic baskets four hours ahead of time. That was most unlike our audiences in the US and Canada who, as I have mentioned, were rarely on time. I asked a stagehand why the audience had arrived so early and he said, 'For the people of Trinidad, Lataji is like a goddess. People literally worship her and arrived here hours ahead to make sure they don't miss a single moment of her singing.'

I was most surprised to also see our local organizer comfortably seated in the venue with his family. He looked relaxed and totally at ease unlike the US organizers I knew who would be running around frantically before a show and seldom having the time to enjoy it.

The private secretary to the president of Trinidad, Mrs N. McNeil, welcomed the audience and introduced Lataji, who bowed graciously, and as usual, touched the podium in a sign of respect, took off her chappals and walked onto the stage to greet the audience. The audience rose to their feet and their rapturous applause could be heard for miles around. Although the people of Indian origin who had come to see her had settled in the Caribbean for generations, and some no longer spoke Hindi, they nevertheless knew her songs. The impact she has on so many millions is immeasurable. When she sang '*Main tulsi tere aangan ki*' and '*Rahen naa rahen hum*', you could hardly hear her for the clapping.

Our next stop was Georgetown in Guyana. It was home turf to us. Our local sponsors, Kenneth Persaud, Vic Insanally and Butch Paramanand, had planned three shows to take place on Friday, 3 October, at the National Cultural Center; Sunday, 5 October, at Georgetown's National Park; and Wednesday, 8 October, at the Albion Sports Complex in Corentyne, which was a boat ride away.

The word had spread. Lata Mangeshkar was coming! The day of her arrival, 1 October

1980, was declared a public holiday. The whole town seemed to have gathered at Georgetown's Timehri International Airport (renamed Cheddi Jagan International Airport). The crowds chanted, 'Lataji, welcome!' 'Lataji, welcome!' She was escorted by a motorcade and news of her arrival was broadcast live over the radio.

Thousands and thousands of people lined both sides of the road. They were not only Indians, but people of all races. As her car passed, many threw flowers in her direction. People waved their hands furiously while others ran alongside the motorcade. Her fans were so eager to catch a glimpse of her that some even climbed onto tree branches to get a better view. In an interview in the local press, Lataji said, 'I have never experienced such crowds outside India. I am deeply touched by everyone who has come here to see me.'

When we reached the centre of Georgetown and stopped at the St George's Cathedral, Lataji got out of the car, and the crowd surged forward.

An old dream was being fulfilled. The mayor of Georgetown presented her with the key to the city. In the background, a band was playing the melody, '*Gumnaam hai koi*'. I was not sure that it was an appropriate song for the occasion, but as we went towards the car, Lataji turned to me and said, 'Did you hear the band? It seems that I will have to sing that too.'

Lataji was invited to stay at a government house reserved for foreign dignitaries, heads of states and prime ministers. The Guyanese press reported in great detail the welcome that she received. The Indian high commissioner was the guest of honour at a crowded function that was held on 2 October at the Indian Culture Center, to coincide with Mahatma Gandhi's birth anniversary.

When Lataji sang at the National Cultural Center concert, the audience went wild with enthusiasm. They greeted the opening bars of each song with enthusiastic applause. Rashid Osman of the *Guyana Chronicle* wrote: 'More than a generation of lovers of Indian music in Guyana are familiar with her lilting voice through a torrent of songs on the soundtracks of hundreds of movies ... last Friday, listening to the very songs directly from their source – 50-year-old Lata, matronly and standing in calm repose – proved to be a tremendously exciting experience ... even if she were to stop singing, Lata the legend is so firmly entrenched that the legend would go on and on.'

From Georgetown we went to Suriname. It was then under president's rule and although a night-time curfew had been imposed in the capital, Paramaribo, we were given special permission to move around at night if we so chose to.

My tour partner, Dr Haren Gandhi, a gifted inventor and engineer, was noted for his work in automotive exhaust catalyst technology. In 2003, he won the National Medal of Technology and Innovation award, the highest honour awarded to inventors by the US president. Haren was obsessed with music and so he became my partner in organizing Lataji's concerts in North

America, West Indies and Fiji. Haren was not driven by financial gain but worked for the sheer pleasure of spending time with great musical personalities like Lataji, Mukeshji, Kishore Kumar and Manna Dey.

As I write this book, memories come back of how Haren Gandhi made sure he fulfilled a simple request that Lataji made of him in Suriname. Everyone knew that Lataji loved hot jalebis, and one day she asked if jalebis and samosas could be arranged for breakfast for her co-singers, musicians and for herself. This task was given to Haren Gandhi. At 8.30 in the morning, on the day after the big concert, Dr Gandhi miraculously had them cooked and packed and went from room to room, down endless hotel corridors, delivering Lataji's choice of breakfast.

Lataji was amazed and asked Haren, 'How did you manage it? You don't even know this city.' Haren beamed from ear to ear and replied, 'How could I not arrange samosas and jalebis if you wanted them? Actually, I contacted the

Hare Krishna Society and they made them for us.' Dr Haren Gandhi was so important in his own field and yet made this very simple request his mission.

During our stay in Suriname, Lataji was awarded an honorary citizenship of the Republic of Suriname. And as expected, an enthusiastic crowd of 10,000 people came to see her sing on stage.

Three years later, in 1983, another adventurous journey awaited us. Lataji had just completed her Australian show at the Sydney Opera House and a show in New Zealand when we persuaded her to stop over in Fiji en route to America.

There was a large number of people of Indian origin living in Fiji. It was a new and unexplored territory for us. But once again, with the help of Dr Haren Gandhi and Raj Sheth, we planned two shows in the Fijian capital, Suva, on 26 and 27 March 1983, a third show in Ba on 29 March and a fourth show at Prince Charles Park in Nadi on 30 March.

As Raj Sheth and I were getting ready to fly to the Fiji Islands, we heard news that the devastating cyclone Oscar had struck and the city of Nadi was the hardest hit. The hotel where we were going to stay was badly damaged. Nadi was without electricity and the streets were flooded. Haren and I arrived in Suva on 15 March, and were advised to move the Nadi show to Lautoka. We kept Lataji informed of the situation. It was time to take some hard decisions. When Lataji heard about the devastation, she immediately decided to make a donation of $10,000 for the Fijian people and proposed to give the cheque to the mayor of Nadi on arrival.

Lataji flew to the Nausori airport from Australia. The airport is a thirty-minute drive from the capital Suva. When we reached the airport, the airport manager asked us where we would like the plane to be parked. We were taken aback. The Fijians were so devoted to Lata Mangeshkar that they went out of their way to show it. When the aircraft landed, the pilot was directed to park right outside the main arrival gate. As soon as the doors opened and Lataji stepped out of the plane, Mayor Manu Patel welcomed her. As she promised, she handed the donation cheque to the mayor.

Lataji talked to the fans who had assembled at the airport and said, 'Namaste, I am touched by your presence here. With your blessings we hope to sing the best we can in your country. I have received more than 300 letters with lists of songs for me to sing. I shall try and sing as many songs as possible. I offer my prayers to the people who have suffered in the cyclone. May this terrible tragedy be soon behind you.' The concerts were, as ever, top-class. Lataji did not disappoint her fans, and I think many older-generation Fijian Indians might still remember those concerts. They meant so much to so many.

In 1983, an amusing incident took place. A close friend, Sudesh Kalia, from Vancouver sent me a flyer. The flyer read: 'YK proudly presents one of the most exquisite entertainment shows of the decade! A dream come true for

Vancouverite fans. The legendary melody queen with your most favourite and adorable superstars Amitabh and Rekha will appear for two shows at the PNE Agrodome, Vancouver on 11 and 12 February 1983. Tickets priced from $20.00 to $30.00 and $10.00 to $15.00.' In block letters the flyer highlighted that fans should book early in order to avoid disappointment. An address and phone number from where to buy the tickets was also provided. One Mr I. Patel of Ambika Foods was named as coordinator.

Knowing that the Vancouver Indians loved Hindi films songs, YK had succeeded in roping in a dozen or so prominent businessmen of the town to associate with him. The bogus scheme may have even reaped a rich harvest of dollars for all we know. Sudesh Kalia, who had helped to organize the Lata Mangeshkar shows in 1975 and 1976, asked me what we should do. He was obviously confused and wondered if the YK team was telling the truth. I assured him that Lataji had no plans of coming to Vancouver, and as a matter of fact, I was organizing the Fiji Islands shows for her at that very moment.

I advised Sudesh that the easiest way to clarify the situation would be for us to have a three-way conference call between Sudesh in Vancouver, Lataji in Mumbai and me in Detroit. When we finally talked, Lataji confirmed to him that she had no plans of coming to Canada as indicated by the YK flyer, and had not authorized anyone to promote a Vancouver concert. She added that she was performing at the Opera House in Sydney in March 1983, and heading to Fiji after that. Sudesh was enraged by the audacity of the YK team or whoever they were. Sudesh had our conference call recorded and played over various South Asian radio stations in Canada. I learned from him later that Lataji's clarification on the whole scam spread like wildfire. YK and associates ran for cover. Those who were duped into buying tickets were advised via a radio message that their money would be refunded.

7

Conjuring Magic with Lata–Kishore: 1985

From the time that we started the concert tours in 1975, we were keen that some of the shows would be non-profit ones, and so three events were in fact charity shows: the first, as I mentioned, was held for the Hare Krishna Society in 1977, the second for the United Way Charity in 1985, and later in 1995, we organized the American Association of Physicians of Indian Origin (AAPI) charity show.

As we were planning the 1985 nine-city tour which was to start in Houston and end

in New York, Lataji received a request from
the Canadian prime minister Brian Mulroney,
through the Canadian embassy in Delhi and
Prime Minister Rajiv Gandhi's office, to ask
her whether she would front a charity show
for United Way, a worldwide organization that
supports education and health. Lataji agreed
and ahead of time, she held a press conference at
Taj Mahal Hotel's Crystal Room on 27 February
1985 to announce the upcoming charity show.
Lataji made the opening statement in English,
'Good morning, Canada, and good evening,
India. I am honoured and proud to address
the people of Toronto and Canada on this
momentous occasion. I believe music is a very
special language that brings people and cultures
closer to one another. People everywhere can
share love and peace through music.'

Via a video link, a Canadian journalist
asked her why she had agreed to the show. She
explained that she found the idea of a charity
event such as 'Do they know it's Christmas?'
held in aid of Ethiopia a very moving gesture. If

artists from the developed world could help the developing world, why should an Indian artist not help the people of Canada? The director of public relations for United Way, John Piper, who came to Mumbai to attend the press conference, presented Lataji with two albums by the very popular Canadian singer Anne Murray and asked her if she could sing an Anne Murray song at the event.

A *Stardust* journalist described the press conference in an amusing way: 'Though I thought I would die of boredom at the press conference organised by United Way, a voluntary aid organisation that was planning to cart Kishore Kumar and Lata Mangeshkar to Canada for a charity show, it turned out to be just the reverse. It was a novel, high-tech press conference with Lata's replies simultaneously telecast to journalists in Canada and vice versa (their voices boomed back so loud and clear on an amplifier, though they were thousands of miles away). But the real surprise of the evening was Latabai herself. As opposed to her stern image, she giggled, blushed like a college girl and happily lapped up all the compliments that the Pakistanis, Canadians, and Sikhs out there paid her. In fact, she so charmed the press on both sides of the ocean that when the Bombay scribes were invited to pose questions, except for one freelancer, all sat dumbstruck!'

Before the charity event took place, our tour kicked off on 24 May 1985 in Houston at the Theatre Southwest. The exceptional singing and unpredictable humour kept the audience totally enthralled. Lata Mangeshkar and Kishore Kumar weaved their magic. As singers and performers, their personalities were poles apart. Conductor and arranger Anil Mohile has said perceptively, 'When Lataji sings, she follows the musicians and when Kishore Kumar sings, the musicians follow him.'

Another insightful description of these two great artists came from the writer, Dr Punita Bhatt: 'She is the living legend, he is the melodious madcap. She is simply the voice, he is the singer–actor–producer–director–

writer–lyricist, all rolled into one. She is reserved but cordial, he is reserved and aloof. On stage together, she stands to one side, her glasses perched on her nose, rendering deeply emotional songs with hardly any expression; he stalks the stage, prances about, clowns, creating a rapport with anything that moves. In professional style and personal manner, Lata Mangeshkar and Kishore Kumar are the fish and fowl of the music industry. They have little in common but their music. Yet, whenever they have teamed up together for stage shows, the totality is greater than the sum of its parts.'

Indeed, Kishore Kumar did not just walk onto the stage but pranced on it. With great flair and an air of the theatrical, he would say as he stepped onto the stage, '*Pyaare doston, sangeet premiyon, mere naana naaniyon, mere maama maamiyon, mere bachche bachchiyon, mere daada daadiyon, mere kaaka kaakiyon, aap sab ko Kishore Kumar Khandwa-wale ka namaskar!*' (An attempt at translation without the rhyme: Dear friends, lovers of music. My maternal grandpas and grandmas, my maternal uncles and aunts, my boys and girls, my paternal grandpas and grandmas, my paternal uncles and aunts – to everyone here – greetings from the man from Khandwa!)

Peals of laughter filled the auditorium and the same reaction repeated itself in every city to Kishore-da's introduction. He then went onto sing his old popular songs and the applause never stopped. Lataji's niece, the actress Padmini Kolhapure, came on stage to say a few words about these two legends. Then came the time for the duets.

It was just amazing to watch Lataji and Kishore-da in action. Their famous impromptu wit had the audience in splits. '*Ab aap ke saamne ek aur duet pesh karenge. Lata bataaengi nahin wo kaun sa duet hai.*' (We are going to sing another duet for you, but Lata won't tell you which one it is.) They started by singing '*Shaayad meri shaadi ka khayal dil mein aaya hai*', and seamlessly they weaved in two other duets, ending with:

Lata: *Piya, dekho diye jalte hain* (Sweetheart, look! The night lamps have now been lit)

Kishore: *Bujha dete hain* (So let me put them out)

Lata: *Achchha to hum chalte hain* (Well, then I had better be going)

As she left the stage, Kishore-da looked startled and said, 'Lata has left! You guys [the audience] do not desert me too. Now I will sing a song that I sang in playback for the Maha-Guru, Dev Anand.' He then went onto sing '*Dukhi mann mere*'.

On 27 May at the Berkeley Community Theater show in San Francisco, Lataji described her relationship with Kishore in a mischievous way, '*Main unhe Dada kehti hoon. Bangali mein Dada yaane bade bhai, aur Marathi mein dada yaane gunda.*' (I call him 'Dada'. In Bengali, Dada means brother, and in Marathi, Dada means gangster.) With equal mischief, Kishore retorted, '*Arrey Lata ne to mujhe gunda keh diya*.' (Hear that? Lata just called me a gangster.)

The United Way charity event was scheduled for 9 June 1985, and in addition to our team of singers, Lataji was keen to have Dilip Kumar introduce her on the night as he had in 1974 at the Royal Albert Hall. Much to our delight, Dilip Kumar agreed and said he and his wife Saira Banu would join us in Toronto.

Before our show in Toronto, we flew to Washington DC on Tuesday, 4 June. Under the banner of Manoranjan Enterprises, it was Dr Punita Bhatt who organized all the Lata Mangeshkar concerts in Washington DC, starting in 1975 through to 1995. As I have mentioned, Punita Bhatt is a fine writer and most knowledgeable about Indian cinema. She has aptly described in this long passage her feelings about Lataji's voice and her experience of the Lata–Kishore concert in Washington DC.

❖

'The voice was God's gift to her; what she made of it was her gift to God. The nine-city concert tour of America and Canada in 1985 was an undoubted triumph, both critically and commercially. Here, in Washington, for example, we saw for ourselves, legions of fans pouring into the city during the weekend of the concert from distances as great as several hundred miles. They came from Pennsylvania, Massachusetts, North and South Carolina, and even as far away as Georgia and Alabama in the south. They came in pairs, families, small groups, and large ones; they came by cars, vans, chartered buses, and in one case, even a chartered airplane. By showtime the audience was so keyed up with excitement that they did, spontaneously, what few showbiz audiences are known to have done; they gave both Lata and Kishore standing ovations before either artiste had even opened his or her mouth to sing. This was history made in public. What happened the day after the Washington concert was historic in a different way. Lata had agreed to tape an interview for a New York-based Indian television programme that day. Kishore, notorious for his aversion towards the press, had been persuaded as well – or so it seemed at the time.'

Punita Bhatt went onto describe to me what happened next: 'The interview was arranged in a suite at Washington's famous Watergate Hotel where the artistes were staying. Lata arrived early and completed her own segment promptly. Kishore walked in twirling a single yellow rose in his hand. He took one look at the set-up – the bright lights, the camera crew, and the interviewer Kiran Vairale. He backed into the suite's kitchenette. From there he refused to budge. Inside he conducted a running monologue while a couple of my friends and I kept him company. Something seemed to have upset him, but it wasn't clear what. His sole condition to emerge from the kitchen was conveyed through us to Lata who was standing outside; she would have to interview him! Lata gamely agreed. Kishore came out and became the very picture of amiable cooperation.'

Punita Bhatt continued with her fascinating account which gave me a real insight into the kind of relationship Kishore-da and Lataji shared. 'The result of this strange twist is a wonderfully refreshing exchange between the two singers. Lata, the questioner, exhibits the aplomb of a seasoned reporter, Kishore responds, disarmingly at times, with a remarkable tendency towards a train-of-consciousness thought process. Asked about his favourite music director, he begins with his first encounter with Lata.

Kishore: When I first entered the industry – you remember, Lata, how you and I first met? We happened to be travelling in the same train one day. You looked at me, I looked at you; you got off at Malad, I got off at Malad; you got into a tanga, I got into a tanga; you reached Bombay Talkies, so did I. You were convinced I was following you. You had come for a song recording with music director Khemchand Prakash, and so had I. The film was *Ziddi*.

Lata: Tell me, how do you like performing on stage with me? Only the truth, please.

Kishore: I love it. I just worry about one thing, you are so reserved and I tend to clown around a lot, so I wonder if I am offending you.

Lata: You see, I have a problem too, I can't run around all over the place and sing.

Kishore: No, Lata, your style is perfect for you. Since I was an actor before I became a full-time singer, the audience expects me to move around and dance, and I try to give them double pleasure!

'Asked about his hobbies, he tells of his need for solitude even as a child. Speaking about the late music director Khemchand Prakash, he takes a swipe at brother Ashok Kumar's efforts at singing. His answers are interspersed with lines of poetry, bits of song and revealing thoughts on life, loneliness and death.

Lata: Do you feel you are happy now?

Kishore: I am very happy. By the grace of God, I want nothing. If there is anything I want, it is to return back home, home is Khandwa, Madhya Pradesh. I hear it calling me. This would be my last wish. K.L. Saigal had the same desire, and he too returned to his native place. Did you know he often used to go and sit in a shamshan? When asked why, he replied: "This after all is my final destination. This is my mandir, this is my masjid."

After our Washington show we flew to Toronto. As soon as we came through customs at the Pearson International Airport, both Lataji and Kishore-da were greeted by several hundred keen fans, many of whom had taken time off work to be there. Even the mayor of Toronto was there to personally welcome everyone. Amidst rousing applause, the mayor declared 9 June 1985 the 'South Asian Day'. Lataji thanked United Way for inviting her to raise funds for a charitable cause, but it was the magnetic Kishore Kumar who spoke in his characteristic style and joked around the most with the journalists present.

Our stay in Toronto was going to be an unusually long one, as we planned to leave the city only on 13 June. Lataji needed more time for rehearsals, and to work on the Anne Murray song that she was going to sing. Furthermore, apart from her usual musicians, fifteen Canadian musicians were added to the orchestra, and they needed to work alongside the Indian musicians. The rehearsals were particularly interesting as all the musicians conversed together, discussing how they would play Hindi film music.

It was surprising to see Kishore Kumar there, as he seldom rehearsed. But this time, Lataji and he rehearsed some of their duets. At the end of the session, to everyone's delight, Kishore-da did a perfect imitation of one of S.D. Burman's famous songs, '*Dheere se jaana bagiyan mein*'.

Harold Ballard of Maple Leaf Gardens did not charge for the venue of the United Way show. And at last the night of the big event arrived. The show was about to start when I realized that I did not have a front-row seat for Saira Banu. All the seats were already occupied. I was in a very awkward situation. I had a ticket for the fifteenth row but could not ask her to sit there. So I requested her to follow me backstage and arranged for a chair right near the stage from where she could very comfortably watch and hear Dilip Saab speak. This may seem like a trivial incident to most, but on the night, and till I found a solution, it felt like the end of the world for me. Organizing tours are full of such moments of crisis and panic – incidents that are wonderful when you recount them later to friends, but heart-stopping while they are unfolding in reality.

Backstage and ready for the start of the show, Dilip Kumar asked Lataji if we could delay his entry a little so that people who were still in the lobby or stuck in traffic would have the time to take their seats. He believed that the auditorium should be full before he came on stage. Lataji paused for a minute, and then came up with a solution. She said the curtain should go up as per schedule; however, her musicians would play a few tunes to give the audience the time to settle down.

The orchestra played some popular melodies while the auditorium filled to capacity. Padmini Kolhapure was the first on stage and introduced Dilip Kumar to the honourable premier of the province of Ontario, the many special guests and the vast audience. That's when Dilip Saab made his entry. The audience erupted with delight, and as expected, they gave him a standing ovation. Few Indian actors have had the continuing respect and adoration that Dilip Kumar had enjoyed for decades.

Dilip Kumar introduced Lataji as his little sister. Because the audience was made up of both South Asians and Canadians, he spoke in a mix of English and Urdu, 'What can I say about Lataji? During the early 1950s, whenever we would sit down for lunch, I used to call her 'ladki', and even now she is a little girl to me. Today I feel proud of this little girl and glad that she has made me a part of this great charitable event. It is not only I, but all the people of Indian origin who are here today, and all Indians are proud that an artiste of a developing country like India could raise funds in the developed world for an organization like United Way of Canada.'

Lataji responded by saying that how grateful she was to Dilip Kumar who never refused anything she ever asked of him, and when she requested him to come to Canada, as usual he had agreed. Saira Banu then came on the stage and asked Lataji to sing her favourite song from *Junglee*: '*Ehsaan tera hoga mujh par*'.

The Anne Murray song that Lataji had decided to sing was the very popular '*You needed me*'. Before Lataji started, I could feel my heart racing. How would this largely Canadian audience react to a song that was so familiar to them? As Lataji hit the first note, it sounded as though she had been born to sing that song. Her diction, her pauses, the way she held a note – she gave a perfect performance of a touching song. I wondered what Anne Murray would have made of Lataji's rendition. We had invited Anne Murray to attend the charity show, but she was out of the country. Just after intermission, the six-year-old Sarah Whiting, who had lost a leg to cancer, presented Lataji with a medallion and flowers from Toronto's South Asian community and the United Way charity. The audience cheered wholeheartedly.

In the show's closing remarks, the president of the Toronto chapter of United Way, Gordon Cressy, emphasized the importance of Lataji's presence in Toronto. 'This truly is a magic moment for Toronto. This has proved Toronto is not only an Anglo-Saxon city. But people from other cultures are ready to stand up and support the city they live in. The concert has united Hindus, Muslims, Christians, Sikhs, Buddhists and people who have roots in African and East and West Indian countries as well. This wonderful lady of song brings things above religion and politics and joins us all as one.'

The United Way charity made a great success of the responsibility of organizing the Toronto show. We met our target of raising $150,000. The donation was seen as an unusual gesture and so it made front-page news in *The Toronto Sun*. As Dilip Kumar had pointed out, I am sure this was the first time a singer from a developing country had donated funds to the developed world.

Dilip Kumar and Saira Banu were scheduled to leave for India straight after our show. Fortunately for us, and possibly because he so enjoyed the event, they decided to stay on and tour with us to New York, Chicago and Detroit.

We had another surprise for the Detroit audience – and that was the guest appearance of Sunil Dutt. Introducing Sunil Dutt, Lataji said that he was not only a star but a wonderful human being too. She also spoke about the charity work that Sunil Dutt was involved in, and added, as a Congress MP, he had spoken in parliament on behalf of the film industry on several occasions.

In response, Sunil Dutt described Lataji as an unusually liberated woman who managed to make a mark in her profession despite the era in which she began working in films, an era that did not favour working women. He then added, '*Main apne guru se milwaaunga – film* Padosan *mein mujhe gaana sikhaane ki koshish ki magar main seekh na saka.*' (Now I would like to introduce my guru to you. In the film *Padosan*, he tried to teach me how to sing, but I couldn't learn.)

This was the cue for Kishore Kumar to make his entry. Knowing that Sunil Dutt was an influential MP, Kishore-da joked, '*Bhole, guru ki ab ek hi darkhwast hai … mujhe* income tax *se bachaalo.*' (Bhole, your guru has only one request, save me from income tax.)

After Kishore Kumar's performance, Dilip Kumar was to go on next. A few minutes before his curtain call, I saw him pacing up and down backstage. He seemed somewhat nervous. Nargisji, who happened to see him, asked, 'How are you, handsome?' It was so charming to hear one icon talking to another like that!

The other surprise presence at the Detroit show was the most special person in Lataji's life, her mother, Mai Mangeshkar. She sat in the first row and when the spotlight was directed to her, the audience clapped vigorously.

A week before the final 1985 show on 22 June in New York, we heard that the Madison Square Garden event (23,000 seater) was completely sold out. On the evening of the performance, the streets around MSG were bursting with South Asian fans who had come to see the artists as they came out of their limousines. There was a carnival type of atmosphere. The other major thrill for the audience was Dilip Kumar's appearance. Another nice moment of the concert was hearing Kishore-da and his son, Amit Kumar, sing *Sholay*'s hit, '*Ye dosti*'.

The last number that Kishore Kumar usually sang at every show was '*Eena meena deeka*'. He brought the house down, jumping around, lying flat on the stage, and clowning till the audience went hysterical. I always wondered how anyone would be able to follow such an act. But then Lataji came on and sang an alaap, and the audience went totally quiet. She followed the alaap with '*Sheesha ho ya dil ho toot jaata hai*'. Her final song of the evening was '*Ae mere watan ke logon*'. Poet Pradeep's patriotic song had famously brought tears to the eyes of Pandit Nehru in 1962 when he had heard Lataji sing it in Delhi. Here, the enthusiastic audience chanted 'Jai Hind' as all the artists including Kishore Kumar, Leena Chandavarkar, Dilip Kumar, Saira Banu, Usha Mangeshkar, Padmini Kolhapure and Amit Kumar joined Lataji on the stage for a last bow.

8

New Voices: 1987 and 1995

By the late 1980s, the audience in the USA and
Canada was changing. Younger audiences made
up of the second and now third generations
of South Asians were filling the auditoriums.
To meet the demands of younger fans, new
singers were included in the mix. And so
along with Nitin Mukesh, Shabbir Kumar and
Suresh Wadkar became part of the 1987 tour.
In addition, three backup singers came from
India, as Lataji planned to sing 'Ghar aaya
mera pardesi' and other songs that needed a
chorus. Two young stars, Rajeev Kapoor and

Mukesh at the Niagara Falls on a day off during his May 1973 concert organized by Mohan Deora and team.

At the Rose Bowl Parade, Pasadena, California. 1 January 1977. The Rose Bowl Parade is a traditional event in America's New Year celebrations.

Lata Mangeshkar and her team stayed at the Hare Krishna Temple apartment complex, Los Angeles. 21 January 1977.

Live intercontinental press conference at the Crystal Room of Taj Mahal Hotel in Mumbai for the United Way charity event, 1985.

With Kishore Kumar, Usha Mangeshkar and their team of musicians. Backstage at Madison Square Garden, New York. 22 June 1985.

Backstage
with Sunil Dutt
who made a
guest appearance
at Detroit's Cobo
Arena show.
16 June 1985.

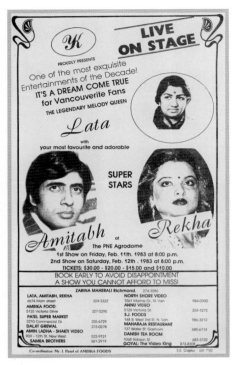

The popularity of the shows attracted fraudsters and scams. Tickets sold for this fictitious show were finally refunded.

A proud moment to see the Lata–Kishore concert sold out at Madison Square Garden, New York. 22 June 1985.

Audiences came in their thousands to see Lata Mangeshkar in both America and Canada.

Photographing her young niece Rachana in the Deora home. Sister Meena also in the frame.

Cooking a Christmas dinner with Suvarna Deora. She regarded the Deora home as a second home.

Wearing Mohan Deora's coat and gloves, she braces herself for the cold Detroit winter. 17 January 1977.

Rehearsing at the Ford Auditorium, Detroit, some hours before curtain call. 16 June1985.

Lata Mangeshkar was presented with an honorary doctorate by York University in Toronto. 20 September 1995.

With Suvarna Deora and Waheeda Rehman in the Deora home. October 1995.

With the Clintons.
Chicago, June 1995.

With the brilliant Kishore Kumar.

On stage with sister Usha Mangeshkar at Detroit's Cobo Arena. 16 June 1985.

Mr and Mrs Raj Kapoor at
the New York show.
25 May 1975.

At the United Way
charity concert,
an emotional
Lata Mangeshkar
held cancer victim
Sarah in her arms.

Lata Mangeshkar at her favourite casino Belagio (l to r) with sister Usha, niece Radha, Arundhati, Suvarna Deora, casino manager and sister Meena.

Lata Mangeshkar with Mohan Deora's son Sunit and Vishakha at their engagement. June 2000.

With Mohan and Suvarna Deora. The Deoras moved from Birmingham, Michigan, to nearby Troy, another suburb of Detroit in 1979.

With Suvarna and Mohan Deora, backstage at Detroit's Cobo Arena. 16 June 1985. Their friendship lasted a lifetime.

Mandakini, who had become popular after the release of *Ram Teri Ganga Maili*, were invited to attend the New York and Toronto concerts.

Accompanied by the younger set of co-singers, Lataji sang a variety of duets that she had originally recorded with her peer group. She sang her old Mukesh duets with Nitin Mukesh; with Shabbir Kumar she sang many memorable Rafi Saab duets; and when it came to Suresh Wadkar, they chose to sing the popular songs of the 1980s. Lataji entertained the audience with her usual ease, while Rajeev Kapoor imitated his father Raj Kapoor in the movie *Shree 420*. Mandakini greeted everyone in her sweet voice, requesting Lataji to sing '*Sun saahiba sun*'.

In Toronto, I heard that Zeenat Aman was in town and requested her to join us and she happily obliged. Surprise guests never failed to excite the audience. And Zeenat Aman was a big star, charming and glamorous.

Then followed an eight-year gap without any tours or concerts. Finally in 1995, we announced a seven-city tour at a press conference, moderated by Lataji herself, at the Gaylord Banquet Hall in Los Angeles on 23 December 1994. Bhallinder Bhalla of Super Entertainment had signed a contract with me and they were the organizers of the LA show. Sanjeev Kohli (son of the wonderful composer Madan Mohan), who, at that time, was working as a consultant to HMV, and I were also present at the press conference. An Indian journalist asked Lataji why she only sang on stage and did not dance. She replied with a laugh, 'No, no, I can't dance on stage as some singers do. Do people who are romancing dance in real life?' Lataji listed the other artists who would accompany her, including S.P. Balasubramaniam, the reigning male singer of the era. We announced that the ever-graceful Waheeda Rehman would introduce Lataji and that went down very well. In the question–answer session, some journalists asked Lataji the usual questions, and she answered them patiently. She also said how much she believed in charity, and that giving should be a secret act, a 'guptdaan' – the left hand should not know what the right hand has given.

By the 1990s, stage production and design had greatly improved thanks to new technologies, and so we decided to include an audio-visual presentation. We also developed a new marketing strategy aimed at young South Asians. Flyers were printed and Lataji's fans were asked to choose their top ten Lata songs that they would like her to sing during the show. The tour was described as a Christmas gift for her fans in America.

We had almost twenty years of experience organizing the tours, but there was always room for improving the technical standards. We wanted the 1995 shows to be remembered as the concerts of the century. Lataji agreed that the Detroit show, scheduled on 1 October 1995, would be, as promised, a fund-raiser for AAPI. Lataji was clear that she wanted a charity associated with health care. She often said that if she had not become a singer, and had been formally educated, she would have liked to become a doctor. She believed people should have the best medical treatment, and it is therefore not surprising that in 2002, she opened a hospital in Pune in the name of her father, Deenanath Mangeshkar.

In 1994, the Rajshri production *Hum Aapke Hain Koun… !* was breaking records in India, and the soundtrack was a major part of the movie's attraction. The most popular song of the year was Lataji's *'Didi tera devar deewana'.* It was a rage in India; and in America, South Asians just loved that song. This made us wonder if the 1995 tour should be called 'Didi Tera America Deewana'. Though the title may have worked, we changed our minds because it wasn't just America that was crazy about Lata Mangeshkar, it was more like half the world was.

Our flyers bore fruit and over 10,000 fans responded with a list of top ten songs that they wanted Lataji to sing. Topping the selection was *'Aayega aanewala'* followed by *'Didi tera devar deewana'.* It suddenly occurred to me that the tour could have a theme: Madhubala to Madhuri. With that in mind, Sanjeev Kohli created a short audio-visual programme of haunting film clips that would play on the backdrop of the stage with images of actresses over generations.

In May 1995, I got a call from Dr Bhimsen Rao who told me that the National Convention of Doctors of Indian Origin organized by the AAPI was going to be held in Chicago in June. They had just received confirmation from the White House that President Bill Clinton would speak at the convention. Dr Rao was very keen that Lataji attend the event and meet the US president. Dr Rao assured us that she would not need to perform, but only be present.

I called Lataji in Mumbai and she agreed to fly to Chicago. Dr Rao was delighted. Shortly after that, I heard the sad news that Mai Mangeshkar had passed away on 16 June 1995. Lataji was devastated. The meeting with Bill Clinton had been confirmed but it happened to fall on the thirteenth day of mourning for the Mangeshkars. It was very difficult for

Lataji to think of leaving her family at such a time, but her family insisted that she honour her commitment.

Accompanied by her niece Rachana, and S.P. Balasubramaniam, Lataji arrived at Chicago for the convention. Dr Rao and the APPI members took her to meet President Clinton and his wife Hillary. Punita Bhatt later interviewed Lataji about that meeting: 'S.P. Balasubramaniam and I were invited into the room where the president and Mrs Clinton were waiting. They said they had heard a lot about me. I was honoured to hear that. Mrs Clinton spoke of her recent trip to India and said how much she had enjoyed it. She added that after the next election, she would like to take her husband to India. Mr Balasubramaniam joked, "In that case we may get to sing for you." I told them that President Clinton had many admirers back home. He is also a musician and I have seen clips of him playing the saxophone. The reason I wanted to meet him was not only because he was the American president but because he was a musician too. I wanted to tell him that, but hesitated. I enjoyed meeting them both.'

Lata Mangeshkar began her seven-city tour of North America with a sellout concert at Nassau Coliseum in Long Island, New York, on 16 September 1995. It was attended by an excited audience of 18,000, while Kanu Chauhan, the local organizer, had to turn away 3,000 very disappointed fans.

As we were getting ready for the Nassau Coliseum show, the stage manager came to me and asked, 'Sir, what time do you start?'

'As announced, 7.38 p.m.,' I said.

He gave me a quizzical look and repeated, 'What time will you actually start the show? None of the Indian shows we've had here have ever started on time.'

I was a little irritated and pulled out my wallet and said, 'Want a bet? If the show does not start on time, you win and you get to keep the wallet. If it starts on time, you lose. What will you pay me?'

The manager got the message and rephrased his question, more politely this time, 'Who is this lady in white? She has a full house and starts the show on time?'

I blurted out vehemently, 'The lady in white is called Lata Mangeshkar.'

The manager of the Nassau Coliseum lost his bet and the show began as scheduled. Waheeda Rehman introduced Lataji saying, 'She is the greatest and most dedicated artist I have ever met.' When the beautiful actress stepped off the stage, Lataji sang '*Kaanton se kheench ke ye aanchal*'. The audience went ballistic.

Our next concert was at SkyDome (renamed the Rogers Center) in Toronto on 24 September. The event was described in the magazine *Law of Attraction*: 'SkyDome resounds with Lata Mangeshkar's peerless voice as 27,000 fans relive 50 years of film music.'

We had chosen the prestigious Fox Theater in Detroit for the AAPI/MAPI charity concert. This was the first time that an Indian popular singer was to perform there. The Fox is considered a national heritage landmark and incredible musicians and singers have performed there, including Joe Williams, the Count Basie Orchestra, Elvis Presley, Frank Sinatra, Sammy Davis Jr and Liza Minnelli. In 1988, the American billionaire Mike Ilitch and his wife acquired the theatre and had it renovated.

My friend and partner for the 1995 Lata–S.P. Balasubramaniam concert, Narendra Sheth, also happened to be my associate in 1976, the year in which Mukeshji had passed away and in 1980 for the Lata–Manna Dey tour. Narendra Sheth recalled how we had raised funds that night: 'Lataji came to Detroit for a fabulous concert held at the prestigious Fox Theater in downtown Detroit on 1 October 1995. This show was a charity event sponsored by the American Association of Physicians of Indian Origin. Mohan Deora, the national organizer of the show, asked me to be the local organizer. Even though the ticket prices were considerably high in order for us to raise funds (tickets scaled from $35 to $500 each), the theatre was completely sold out. Over 5,000 people waited anxiously to see Lataji perform.'

Narendra added: 'Detroit had a relatively small Indian community, but this was a record-breaking event. Never before had we seen so many people of Indian origin at the Fox. We netted a profit of over $300,000; and in 1995, almost twenty years ago, that was a huge amount of money. The funds were used to support eleven free medical clinics in India and to provide medical care to people who were poor. Because of this humanitarian cause, Lataji did not charge a dollar for the concert and wholly supported AAPI's cause. May God give Lataji many years of healthy life.'

Narendra made a very insightful comment about Lataji that I would like to share: 'One very important thing I learned observing Lataji is that the sweetness of her speaking voice is like the perfect "sur" of her singing voice. I observed this when I was walking with her to the boarding gate from the entrance of the

Detroit airport. Lataji and I were talking about some aspect of music, and even though she was talking, it sounded as though she was singing. Her speaking voice is that sweet. I came to the conclusion that if the sur is perfect, it would influence the sweet quality of the spoken voice.'

At the 'Madhubala to Madhuri' benefit show, the AAPI president Dr C. Venkat S. Ram, and the chairman, Dr Bhimsen Rao, began the evening by talking about the activities of the charity, and how they worked in poor and remote areas of India, and supplied medical equipment to Indian charitable and educational institutions.

As lovely as ever, Waheeda Rehman entered the stage in a white sari with a red border and greeted the audience, 'Good evening, ladies and gentlemen. I have been given an impossible task – to introduce an artiste of Lataji's stature. Her name itself is her introduction. A wide variety of brilliant composers and gifted lyricists have written the music that she has brought to life. She has lent her voice to actresses for over fifty years – and still does. Music is her life and her voice is indeed a gift from God.'

Lataji began the evening by thanking Waheedaji, adding that she thought Waheedaji was a fine actress and a good human being. Before she sang, she also said, 'Today I am pleased to perform in front of so many doctors. The medical profession is a noble one and I have great respect for it. When I am asked what I would like to be if I were reborn, I always say I want to be a doctor.'

People went crazy. They clapped their hands and stamped their feet. Lataji added, 'I have no words to describe the beauty of the Fox Theater where we are tonight. The song I shall sing, I think, is appropriate for this setting.' '*Jab pyaar kiya to darna kya*' from *Mughal-e-Azam*, a lovely song picturized on Madhubala, which is famous for its spectacular Sheesh Mahal set, was the song she chose. The revolving stage at the theatre enhanced the enjoyment for the audience because people who were seated in different sections of the theatre could have a closer view of Lataji.

Then it was S.P. Balasubramaniam's turn. He dedicated a song to Waheedaji and sang the wonderful Mohammed Rafi number '*Chaudhvin ka chand*'. An old catchy song, '*Lara lappa*' from the 1940s film *Ek Thi Ladki*, composed by the forgotten music director Vinod, energized the audience. It was amazing how fifty-five years after the release of the film, people still remembered that song. It just goes to show how film songs have extended the life of so many movies that would have otherwise been totally forgotten.

Just before the intermission, a small ceremony was held and presentations made. The mayor of Detroit, Dennis Archer, and Mike and Marion Ilitch (the owners of Fox Theater) were invited on stage. Mike Ilitch presented Lataji with a bouquet of flowers and pecked her on the cheek. There was pin-drop silence. With a smile, Lataji gracefully accepted the bouquet. When the mayor presented his bouquet to Balasubramaniam, he said with great wit, 'Let me assure you that I am not going to start a rumour here by kissing you.' His comment was drowned by laughter. The mayor shook hands with Lataji and welcomed her to Detroit.

During the intermission, Mr Ilitch asked me, 'What was going on there? Did I do something wrong?' We reassured him that he did nothing wrong – only that the audience did not expect someone would give Lataji a peck on the cheek.

In the second half of the show, it was time for the theme song 'Madhubala to Madhuri'. Lataji sang a medley, starting with the ever favourite, '*Aayega aanewala*', a song picturized on Madhubala and ending with '*Didi tera devar deewana*', shot on Madhuri Dixit. A montage showing Hindi cinema's great heroines was projected as backdrop, and as the show ended with the rousing '*Vande Mataram*', there was an explosion of joy in the theatre.

We managed to raise a quarter of a million dollars that night for AAPI. The evening after the Detroit concert, I invited Lataji and Waheedaji home for dinner. On the drive to Birmingham where we lived, Waheedaji said, 'If I am born again, I would like to be a singer. Our career as actresses is over when we are above thirty, while singers can sing even at sixty or seventy. Look at Lataji, she can still sing a song for a seventeen-year-old actress.'

It was such an honour for my family and me to have these two great artists home for dinner. I took pictures while my wife, Suvarna, made us a delicious meal.

9

The Final Tour: 1998

Super Entertainment organized Lataji's 1998 tour, although I played an active role as a partner. We did not guess at the time that this would be the last Lata Mangeshkar tour to the USA and Canada.

On 28 September 1998, Lataji turned seventy. She had fifty-six years of an amazing career behind her. Her countless songs and duets have touched, and continue to touch, millions of people across generations and cultures. It was also an important year for the Mangeshkar family because it coincided with the celebration of Deenanath Mangeshkar's birth centenary.

The tours, which had started in 1975, were very special to us. By 1998, we had staged fifty concerts. Through the years, many great artists, including Mukeshji, Kishore Kumar, Nitin Mukesh, S.P. Balasubramaniam, Amit Kumar and a host of younger singers had accompanied her on stage. Her family – Usha, Meena, Hridaynath, Rachana, Adinath, Baijnath and, later, young Radha – was also an integral part of many shows. She had the best actors introducing her, including Dilip Kumar, Raj Kapoor, Amitabh Bachchan, Sunil Dutt, Waheeda Rehman and Farida Jalal.

I gradually discovered that Lataji is not really an introvert. We had initially thought so because she hardly spoke to the audience. The first time she appeared in America in 1975, she was shy and reticent. I still remember her fans in Trinidad and Tobago egging on the quiet Lataji by shouting, 'Lata, say something. Lata, say something!' They were very eager to hear her speaking voice. That said, by 1998, Lataji had almost replaced the master of ceremony. Once she had finished singing the shloka, she interacted with the audience spontaneously and with great ease.

'*Is saal maine film industry mein apne chhappan saal,* fifty-six years, *purey kiye hain. Ho sakta hai ki itne lambe safar ke baad, main gaane mein kuchh galat kar baithun ya sur kuchh upar neeche ho sakte hain, asha hai us bhool ko aap kshama kar denge aur mera gaana aap ussi pyaar se sunenge jo aap chhappan saal se sunte aaye hain.*' (I have completed fifty-six years in the film industry. It is possible that after such a long journey, I might make a mistake while singing, maybe mix up a line or two. I hope you'll forgive me and will listen to my singing with the same affection that you have shown me for the past fifty-six years.)

She came out with another surprise. 'Until now I have been singing songs that you like. But now I shall sing a song that I like. If you like it, please clap. If you don't, please be silent.'

The audience burst out laughing. When they stopped clapping, she sang that beautiful and unusual song from *Anupama*, '*Kuchh dil ne kaha, kuchh bhi nahin*'.

When Lataji invited Sudesh Bhosle on the stage, she explained that he wasn't feeling well and had a fever but insisted on singing. She added that she would trouble him further by asking him to sing a duet with her. They sang together and to the audience's delight, she asked him to impersonate Mukesh, Mohammed Rafi, Hemant Kumar and Kishore Kumar, which he did remarkably well. In between almost every song, Lataji addressed the audience, connecting to everyone in that auditorium. When she spoke of Naushad Ali's composition for the *Andaz* song, '*Uthaye jaa unke situm*', she shared memories of how the song was recorded. 'When I started singing, Naushad Saab came to me and said, "*Is gaane ko gaate samay aap apni bahen Noorjehan ko dhyan mein rakhiye.*"' (When you sing this song, keep your sister Noorjehan in mind.)

Lataji asked herself, '*Kya meri pehchaan Noorjehan se hai? Nahin, meri pehchaan to Lata Mangeshkar honi chaahiye.*' (Should I be an imitator of Noorjehan? No, I should be known as Lata Mangeshkar.) And this is how the world knows her.

The 27 September concert in Chicago at the UIC Pavilion was another successful event. It took place in the middle of the Navratri festivities. Lataji was born on 28 September 1929 at 10.30 p.m. in Indore. We figured out that she would be singing, seventy years later, in front of her 12,000 Chicago fans at about the same time. So we planned a surprise celebration at exactly 10.30 p.m. US time. We kept it a secret from her. As soon as she entered the arena, the entire audience rose to its feet, clapping loudly. After the shloka, Ushaji and she sang a popular Gujarati song, '*Mehndi te vavi malvene ano rang gayo Gujarat re*' (The henna from Malwa has painted Gujarat in its deep colour). Chicago had a very large population from Gujarat and the local organizers were the Patel brothers. When the audience heard the Gujarati song, they went wild. By the end of this lively number almost 12,000 people were on their feet, dancing garba-style. It was a beautiful and heartening sight.

As people were still dancing, the musicians changed the tune and played 'Happy birthday to you!' Lataji's family members and all our backstage team walked onto the stage with signs that read 'Happy Birthday'. Sanjeev Kohli made the following announcement: 'Today at the stroke of midnight in India, Lataji will enter her seventieth year with fifty-six years of singing career behind her!'

Twelve thousand fans sang 'Happy birthday to you, Lataji!' We could see how moved she was but she tried not to show it. She smiled and joined her hands in a 'namaste' and bowed to the audience. She walked across the stage and untied the balloons that floated high up into the auditorium.

The rush of emotion that engulfed Chicago's UIC Pavilion that night was palpable. After the show had ended, we arranged a private party at a lovely restaurant. We wanted to cut a cake and celebrate again. I felt honoured to be present when Lataji turned seventy.

Sanjeev Kohli opened our Sunday, 4 October show at the Universal Amphitheater (renamed Gibson Amphitheater) and introduced the musicians, the conductor, the chorus singers, the sound recordist and the troupe manager. He then invited Farida Jalal to introduce Lataji. We were very pleased that Faridaji had agreed to be part of our 1998 team. A five-time winner of the Filmfare Awards, she is a fine actress who has given wonderful performances in several top Hindi films. I quote some lines from Faridaji's heartfelt introduction, 'Some people consider India behind other countries in terms of progress. It is poor and underdeveloped. This is true to some extent. But when speaking of good singing voices, it is unlikely that there is a country in this world that is richer than ours, because we have that precious diamond who is called Lata Mangeshkar. I will not stand in the way any longer between you and this great artist.

Ladies and gentlemen, it is my privilege to invite the voice of India, the undisputed melody queen of Indian music, Lata Mangeshkar.'

Dressed in her trademark white sari, Lataji stepped onto the stage. The next four hours was all pure music. Sudesh Bhosle and all the members of Lataji's family sang – Hridaynath, her sisters Meena and Usha, Hridaynath's children, Adinath, Baijnath and Radha. The sense that here was a deeply talented musical family dominated the evening. Lataji told the audiences that even her father and grandfather were reputed singers.

The orchestra of over twenty-five instrumentalists and three backup singers (think of the 1975 tour, when she had only five musicians and no backup singers), a large backdrop that changed colours, twin portraits of her parents, the late Master Deenanath and Mai Mangeshkar, sketched by her sister Usha, adorned the stage.

Among the songs that Lataji sang that night were '*Wo bhooli dastaan*' from *Sanjog* composed by Madan Mohan and written by Rajinder Krishan, '*Tere bina zindagi se koi shikwa nahin*', composed by R.D. Burman and written by Gulzar, and '*Mere khwabon mein jo aaye*' from *Dilwale Dulhania Le Jayenge*, composed by Jatin–Lalit and written by Anand Bakshi. Her diamond earrings and gold bangles sparkled as she moved to keep time. Lataji's fondness for diamonds is well known. She told me that she had even studied precious stones, and knows as much about them as a professional jeweller.

She spoke to the audience about the importance of 1998 for the Mangeshkars. 'This year marks my father's birth centenary. All of us – my brother and sisters – have contributed our personal money to create a charity trust called the Deenanath Smruti Pratishthan. The trust has no outside support, but it has managed to build many music halls and helped hundreds of destitute and needy people. Today the organizers of this tour have donated $100,000 to the cause.' A classical vocalist himself, Hridaynath Mangeshkar then sang his own composition from the movie *Lekin*.

The Final Tour: 1998

Following the show in Saddledome in Calgary, Canada, on Sunday 11 October 1998, Brigitte Jobin of *The Calgary Sun* wrote a warm and affectionate piece that had a great title, 'Love that Lata': 'They left the Saddledome last night with grins from ear to ear. About 5,000 fans had gathered to see international superstar Lata Mangeshkar. The seventy-year-old Indian singer has applied her three-octave voice in seventeen different languages – a world record. "She is a legend of our time," said fan Naz Alibhai. "I heard her twenty-eight years ago in Mumbai and her voice is still the same," said fan Jaymal Ruparel. "She is incredible." Ruparel's son Rajen said he didn't grow up listening to her, but he still enjoyed the show. "Her voice is so young," Rajen said.'

When the phone had rung in my condo twenty-three years earlier on 28 September 1974 (coincidentally Lataji's birthday), I could never have imagined that Nandi Duggal's call would set off a chain of events that would change the course of my life. Mukeshji helped me to meet Lataji, she agreed to the tours, we travelled from city to city, from country to country, we lost our dear friend Mukeshji, and most importantly, for over four decades, the friendship between Lata Mangeshkar and my family and me remained intact.

10

Didi and I

Tours and business apart, Lataji has influenced me personally in many ways. The Tulsidas chaupai that she has cited in her tribute album to Mukesh, 'Haani–laabh, jeewan–maran, yash–apyash, vidhi haath' (Loss–profit, life–death, fame–notoriety is all in God's hands) is the guiding principle of my life.

Though she is by nature a reserved person, when Didi (I had started calling her 'Didi' early on in our relationship) accepts someone, the ties that she forms are deep. She is a dependable friend, not a matlabi (driven by self-interest) kind of person. In fact she has a great sense of respect for others. I saw proof of that many times and recall one particular example. We all knew that Didi was a stickler for punctuality, so the shows had to start on time – and somehow we always managed it. That said, a show in Detroit did start late. We were flying from Chicago to Detroit. Chicago is an hour behind Detroit, and when we landed, we forgot to tell Didi to put her watch forward. She arrived at the auditorium at 8 p.m. thinking it was 7 while the start time was 7.35. By the time she went on stage, she had become aware of the mix-up and that she was in fact twenty-five minutes late. She addressed the audience and apologized with great sincerity, even explaining what caused the delay. In all my experience of stars, this was a first.

During those happy years when we spent a lot of time together, I discovered there were some American cities that Didi adored. Whenever she visited the States with the family, on tour or vacation, they made it a point to visit New York and Las Vegas. New York is a city that never sleeps and one is spoilt for choice of how to spend an evening – the best nightclubs, fabulous live music, restaurants and Broadway shows. We used to stay at the New York Hilton Midtown, or sometimes at the Waldorf Astoria, or the Hyatt or the Helmsley Palace Hotel, but the Hilton was her first choice because Fifth Avenue, the shopper's paradise with its designer boutiques, was within walking distance. Didi was very fond of walking in New York and loved the Indian restaurants there. It was either Indian or her second favourite, Chinese cuisine, that we relished night after night.

Las Vegas was the other city where she loved spending time. She was so relaxed there, so at ease with herself. Didi and Suvarna would spend hours in the shopping malls, but Didi did not shop for herself – instead she bought gifts for her family and friends back home in India.

In Las Vegas, there were no deadlines to meet, no pressure of work. Didi walked around her favourite casino, the Bellagio Hotel and Casino, and enjoyed the food there. For someone who has given so much pleasure through her songs to so many millions, it was surprising and heart-warming to see the simple things that gave her pleasure – the excitement was written over her face when she won $100 at a slot machine. Perhaps it was the sound of the dollar coins tumbling out that gave her a thrill. The Bellaggio Fountains, an elaborate watershow, was another great attraction for her. She could watch the watershow again and again.

I once asked her if she would like to stay at Caesars Palace Hotel. It's a very famous place – that's where Frank Sinatra used to sing. But Caesars Palace was not to her liking. She found the hotel room windows too narrow so that she could not enjoy a full view of Vegas. During our travels, I became aware of her love for photography. She was a brilliant photographer and took many pictures.

In June 1997, we stayed at the thirty-storey MGM Grand Hotel Casino. That was the year when the fight between Mike Tyson and Evander Holyfield was going to take place at the MGM Grand Garden Arena. Didi's nephew Adinath was with us and he was keen to see the title bout. We somehow managed to get him a ticket and he headed off.

An hour or so later, we were in the shopping mall when suddenly news of Mike Tyson's ear-biting episode spread. Tyson had bit off part of Holyfield's ear. We heard there was chaos in the arena. We were very concerned for Adinath, so we immediately took a cab and returned to the hotel. When we got there, we found that the police had cordoned off the hotel and blocked all the entrances. This was because the crowds from the big fight had flooded into the hotel lobby and there was pandemonium. We explained to the police officers that we were hotel guests, so they let us through.

We were very worried about Adinath. We assumed that he was still inside the arena, perhaps unable to get out, or worse still, hurt in the near-stampede. It was very difficult to make our way through the crowds, so we advised Didi to go to her room and wait there. I ran towards the arena. There were people everywhere, rushing around frantically. To my great relief, I saw Adinath coming towards me. Thankfully, he was unhurt. We quickly made our way back to the hotel where Didi was waiting anxiously in her room. When Adinath walked in, she let out a sigh of relief. He then had to give us a detailed account of the entire drama. That bout is now a historic event in the world of boxing.

There were other times when Didi and her family would come for a holiday to America and relax in our home. My wife spoilt us by making a variety of dishes. One day she had made some stir-fried rice with tons of red chillies in it. My son, Sunit, who was young at the time sat at the dining table eating the rice. When Didi saw him, she asked Suvarna if she could have some too. Didi? Asking for spicy rice? I was amazed. I thought singers would not eat spicy food to protect their throats. But Didi enjoyed all kinds of food.

The fact that she considers Detroit her second home is, for me, like being blessed by both Saraswati and Lakshmi. I think that she is indeed Saraswati and Lakshmi. I believe Pandit Hari Prasad Chaurasia also felt the same when he once said, 'Generally speaking, people believe that Saraswati and Lakshmi are not supposed to reside together. But then look at Lataji!'

We discovered an endearing thing about Didi and that was her weakness for frozen Coca-Cola. We were once in Atlanta when she called my wife early one morning from her hotel to tell Suvarna that she had visited the Coca-Cola factory the day before. The city mayor had taken her there on a VIP tour. But now she was very worried, 'My throat has packed in and tonight's the show. Lata drank many flavoured Cokes at the Coca-Cola factory. She gulped them down like a kid. The lychee Coke was the best! But what shall I do now?'

It was funny that Didi told the story in the third person: 'Lata' drank many flavoured Cokes'. Suvarna told her not to worry and said she would come straight over. She went to Didi's hotel room armed with all kinds of ingredients: honey, salt, lemon and ginger powder. She instructed Didi to gargle with hot salt water and made her drink a cocktail of the ingredients she took with her. The formula worked and later that afternoon Didi called me to say my wife had performed a miracle and her throat was fine.

During the 1985 concert, we welcomed another honoured guest in our home. Didi brought her mother to stay with us. Everyone called her Mai. Mai became very fond of Suvarna and would even tell her which sari she should wear: a red one was Mai's choice. When the time came for Didi to leave for New York for the next concert, Mai asked, 'Is Bhabhi coming with us?'

'Not now. She'll join us in two days. The children have school.'

Then Mai said she preferred to stay with my wife and later travel with her to New York. Mai once gave Suvarna a beautiful necklace. She still treasures it.

On a trip to Mumbai I learned that Didi had a spiritual guide in Pandit Narendra Sharma. Didi took me to Khar where he lived and introduced us. Panditji was a religious scholar, writer, poet and a lyricist. He wrote some beautiful songs, including '*Satyam Shivam Sundaram*' and '*Jyoti kalash chhalke*'. He was a man of many talents and was also a consultant to B.R. Chopra in the making of the TV series *Mahabharat* for Indian television.

Didi always consulted Panditji about which dates were auspicious for the tour. I did not really believe in astrology, but she took Panditji's advice very seriously. He was in many ways a kind of father figure to her.

I remember we had almost finalized our 1984 tour when Lataji called, 'Mohan Bhaiya, *Panditji keh rehe hain ye saal ka mahurat achchha nahin hai – hamaara show 1985 mein karenge. Unke anusaar woh saal achchha rahega.*' (Panditji says this year is not an auspicious one. Let us postpone the tour to next year. He believes 1985 will be a good year.) So we postponed the tour dates from 1984 to 1985.

It may have been a complete coincidence, but 1984 turned out to be a very traumatic year for India. On 31 October 1984, Prime Minister Indira Gandhi's Sikh bodyguards assassinated her. Considering that Sikhs made up for much of the audience in Canada, and given the tragic circumstances, we would have had to cancel some shows. Condolence meetings were held everywhere for the thousands of innocent Sikhs who were killed in the terrible riots that followed in Delhi and in other Indian cities. When I heard the news, Pandit Narendra Sharma's words came to my mind.

Lataji has changed my life in so many ways. I am from a very modest background. I came to America in 1964 to study and became a nuclear energy consultant. Throughout the time that we were organizing the tours, I had a full-time job. It was demanding, but Didi encouraged me to work hard and to excel. It was she who helped my family to rise socially and prosper; we were lower middle class really. For me, Lataji is indeed Saraswati and Lakshmi. It was thanks to her that I even started a business in India and opened a plywood shop in Vile Parle in Mumbai called Sunit Plywood. She attended the opening of the shop and gave me her blessings. The shop is doing very well.

And if all this was not enough, Didi rescued Suvarna and me when we were stranded in Uttarkashi in June 2013. People will remember the terrible floods and landslides of that year. Over 5,000 people were presumed dead. It was the worst natural disaster since the tsunami in 2004. We had no way of getting out. We had run out of medicine and hope. It was Didi, through the chief minister's office and the Indo-Tibetan Border Police (ITBP) camp heads, who led us to safety.

If I were to describe my feelings for Didi, who now calls me her rakhee brother, it would take me forty-one years – that's how many years I have known her. I believe our friendship deepened over the time that we took our shows across the US and Canada. In a fickle industry like the film industry, such a long relationship is rare, so it makes me proud to think that neither of us has allowed anything to spoil our friendship.

Lataji has treated my family and me as an elder sister would. She still remains an integral part of the Deora family. Come to think of it, amidst the flurry of activity, booking auditoriums, hotels, airline tickets, holding press conferences, making frantic calls and problem solving, I did not realize when Lataji became 'Didi' to me.

Perhaps the turning point in our relationship came just after the very first tour in 1975. Given that the tour was over, Lataji and her family had decided to spend a few days in Canada with Lataji's closest friend Nalini Mhatre. Naliniji lived in Kingston and the Mangeshkars invited me to come along. It was a much-needed break for us all, but more than that, it was a wonderful way of discovering a certain childlike quality of Lataji. She was a bundle of energy. Her stamina was unbeatable. She was on her feet for hours without the slightest trace of fatigue. She was happy to cook for everyone, and happy just to sit and chat with Nalini. Her delightful sense of humour, her simplicity and her contagious smile were so endearing.

But the holiday had to end, and the day came when I had to accompany her to the Montreal airport to say goodbye. As she was boarding the flight to India, a teary-eyed Lataji turned to me and said, 'I have never really known how it feels for a bride to leave her family. I don't like the idea of leaving today. You and your family have become like family to me.' Her words are my most cherished memory. I had a lump in my throat. She stopped me from bowing down to touch her feet in respect. That was the first time I called her Didi.

Appendix

1975 North America Concerts

- Lata Mangeshkar, Mukesh and Usha Mangeshkar
- National organizers: Mohan Deora and Ramesh Shishu
- Master of Ceremony (MC): Ramesh Shishu
- Guest appearance: Raj Kapoor (the Felt Forum, NY)
- Date, venue and local organizer/s:
  - Friday, 9 May, Los Angeles, Shrine Auditorium, Gurudayal Mann
  - Saturday, 10 May, Vancouver (Canada), Pacific Coliseum, Aftab Alam
  - Sunday, 11 May, San Francisco, Oakland Coliseum, Gurudayal Mann
  - Saturday, 17 May, Toronto (Canada), Maple Leaf Gardens, Alam/Jafry/Moin Ansari

- Monday, 19 May, Washington DC, Kennedy Center for the Performing Arts, Dr Punita Bhatt and Praveen Ponda
- Friday, 23 May, Chicago, Civic Opera Hall, Moin Ansari and Keen
- Saturday, 24 May, Detroit, Ford Auditorium, Mohan Deora and Ramesh Shishu
- Sunday, 25 May, New York, Felt Forum (MSG), Moin Ansari and Keen
- Monday, 26 May, New York, Carnegie Hall, Moin Ansari and Keen

1976 North America Concerts

- Lata Mangeshkar, Mukesh and Usha Mangeshkar
- National organizers: Mohan Deora and Dr Sid Mittra
- MC: Dr Sid Mittra
- Date, venue and local organizer/s:
    - Sunday, 1 August, Vancouver (Canada), Queen Elizabeth Hall, Sudesh Kalia
    - Saturday, 7 August, Milwaukee, Performing Arts Center, Adi
    - Sunday, 8 August, Washington DC, Kennedy Center, Dr Punita Bhatt and Praveen Ponda
    - Saturday, 14 August, Houston, Jesse H. Jones Hall for the Performing Arts, Gopal Rana of India Cultural Center
    - Monday, 16 August, Cleveland, Front Row Theater, Cleveland India Association

- Friday, 20 August, Boston, Berkelee Performance Center, Chunawala
- Saturday, 21 August, Montreal, Expo 1967 Theater, India Association of Montreal
- Sunday, 22 August, Toronto, O'Keefe Center, Darshan Sahota
- Friday, 27 August, Detroit, Ford Auditorium, Narendra Sheth (Cancelled because of Mukeshji's death)
- Sunday, 29 August, Philadelphia, Valley Forge Music fair, Jayant-Mala Parmar (Cancelled because of Mukeshji's death)

1977 North America Concerts

- Lata Mangeshkar, Usha Mangeshkar and Nitin Mukesh
- National organizer: Mohan Deora
- MC: Padma Sachdev
- Date, venue and local organizer/s:
  - Saturday, 15 January, New York, Felt Forum (MSG) Jayant Parmar
  - Sunday, 16 January, Philadelphia, Valley Forge Music Fair, Jayant Parmar
  - Saturday, 22 January, Los Angeles, Shrine Auditorium (Charity Concert for Hare Krishna Society)

1980 North America Concerts

- Lata Mangeshkar, Manna Dey and Usha Mangeshkar

- Amitabh Bachchan (Special Appearance in New York and Toronto)
- National organizer: Mohan Deora
- MC: Harish Bhimani
- Date, venue and local organizer/s:
    - Friday, 12 September, Washington, Kennedy Center, Dr Punita Bhatt and Saurabh Ponda
    - Sunday, 14 September, Chicago, Arie Crown, Amir and Anar Rehmat
    - Friday, 19 September, Detroit, Ford Auditorium, Narendra and Suhash Sheth
    - Saturday, 20 September, New York, Felt Forum (MSG), Asha Entertainments, Mahendra Shah and Vipul Shah
    - Sunday, 21 September, Toronto, Maple Leaf Gardens, Darshan Sahota

1980 Concert Tour, the West Indies and South America

- Lata Mangeshkar, Usha Mangeshkar, Nitin Mukesh
- National organizers: Mohan Deora and Dr Haren Gandhi
- MC: Harish Bhimani
- Local organizer/s: Kenneth Persaud, Victor Insanally, Paramanand (Butch)
- Date and venue:
    - 27 and 28 September, Jean Pierre Sports Complex, Port-of-Spain, Trinidad
    - 3, 5 and 7 October, Georgetown (Guyana)
    - 9 October, Paramaribo (Suriname)

1983 Concert Tour, Fiji

- Lata Mangeshkar, Usha Mangeshkar, Nitin Mukesh
- MC: Harish Bhimani
- National organizers: Mohan Deora, Dr Haren Gandhi, Raj Sheth
- Date and venue:
  - 26-27 March, Suva, National Sports Arena
  - 29 March, Ba Sports Stadium
  - 30 March, Nandi, Prince Charles Park

1985 North America Concerts

- Lata Mangeshkar, Kishore Kumar, Usha Mangeshkar and Padmini Kohlapure
- Dilip Kumar and Saira Bano (Special appearance in Chicago, Detroit, Toronto and New York)
- Guest appearance: Sunil Dutt (Detroit)
- National organizers: Mohan Deora, Dr Haren Gandhi and Raj Sheth
- MC: Harish Bhimani
- Date, venue and local organizer/s:
  - Friday, 24 May, Houston, Theater Southwest, Dr Virendra Mathur and Meena Dutt
  - Saturday, 25 May, Los Angeles, Shrine Auditorium, Pramod Mistry and Yakub Dada
  - Monday, 27 May, San Francisco, the Berkeley Community Theater, Arvind Patel
  - Saturday, 1 June, Miami, Omni Auditorium, A. Qureshi
  - Sunday, 2 June, Washington DC Constitution Hall, Dr Punita Bhatt

- Sunday, 9 June, Toronto, Maple Leaf Gardens (Charity Concert for United Way)
- Saturday, 15 June, Chicago, Rosemont Horizon (now Allstate Arena), Syed Majid
- Sunday, 16 June, Detroit, Cobo Arena, Mohan Deora, Dr Haren Gandhi and Raj Sheth
- Saturday, 22 June, New York, Madison Square Main Arena, Shashikant Patel

1987 USA *and Canada Concerts*

- Lata Mangeshkar, Usha Mangeshkar, Nitin Mukesh, Shabbir Kumar and Suresh Wadkar
- Rajeev Kapoor and Mandakini (Special appearances in New York and Toronto)
- Zeenat Aman (Special appearance in Toronto)
- National organizers: Mohan Deora and Dr Haren Gandhi
- MC: Harish Bhimani
- Date, venue and local organizer/s:
  - Thursday, 11 June, Washington DC, Constitution Hall, Dr Punita Bhatt
  - Saturday, 13 June, New York, Madison Square Garden Main Arena, Shashikant Patel
  - Sunday, 14 June, Toronto, Maple Leaf Gardens, Darshan Sahota
  - Friday, 19 June, Atlanta, Civic Opera House, Bhulabhai Patel
  - Saturday, 20 June, Los Angeles, Shrine Auditorium, Saaz Entertainments

- Friday, 26 June, Houston
- Saturday, 27 June, Chicago
- Sunday, 28 June, Detroit, Ford Auditorium, Narendra Sheth

1995 USA and Canada Concerts

- Lata Mangeshkar, Hridaynath Mangeshkar, S.P. Balasubramaniam, Sudesh Bhosle, Usha Mangeshkar
- Special Guest: Waheeda Rehaman
- National organizer: Mohan Deora
- MC: Arundhati
- Date, venue and local organizer/s:
  - Saturday, 16 September, New York, Nassau Coliseum, Kanu Chauhan
  - Sunday, 17 September, Washington DC, Constitution Hall, Dr Punita Bhatt and Saurabh Ponda
  - Sunday, 24 September, Toronto, Skydome, Shan Chandra Shekhar
  - Saturday, 30 September, Chicago, UIC Pavilion, Mayur Ganger
  - Sunday, 1 October, Detroit, Fox Theater (Charity Show for AAPI/MAPI), Narendra Sheth
  - Friday, 6 October, Houston, Hofheinz Pavilion, Alok Kalia
  - Saturday, 7 October, Los Angeles, Shrine Auditorium, Bhallinder Bhalla and Manoj Kaytee

1998 USA and Canada Concerts

- Lata Mangeshkar, Hridaynath Mangeshkar, Usha Mangeshkar, Meena Mangeshkar, Adinath Mangeshkar, Baijnath Mangeshkar, and Radha Mangeshkar, with Sudesh Bhosle
- MC: Farida Jalal
- National organizer: Bhallinder Bhalla and Mohan Deora
- Date, venue and local organizers:
  - Friday, 25 September, Dallas, Bronco Bowl, Jawed Yusuf, Tahir Ali
  - Sunday, 27 September, Chicago, UIC Pavilion, Patel brothers
  - Friday, 2 October, Atlanta, Atlanta Civic Center, Mark Premji
  - Sunday, 4 October, Los Angeles, Universal Amphitheater, Super Entertainment
  - Friday, 9 October, Calgary, Saddledome, Dr Surani
  - Sunday, 11 October, San Francisco, Henry J. Kaiser Convention Center Oakland, Mehta brothers
  - Saturday, 17 October, New York, Nassau Coliseum, Kanu Chauhan